COUNTRIES, REGIONAL STUDIES, TRADING BLOCKS, UNIONS, WORLD ORGANIZATIONS

BRAZIL

CONDITIONS, ISSUES AND U.S. RELATIONS

COUNTRIES, REGIONAL STUDIES, TRADING BLOCKS, UNIONS, WORLD ORGANIZATIONS

Additional books in this series can be found on Nova's website under the Series tab.

Additional e-books in this series can be found on Nova's website under the e-book tab.

COUNTRIES, REGIONAL STUDIES, TRADING BLOCKS, UNIONS, WORLD ORGANIZATIONS

BRAZIL

CONDITIONS, ISSUES AND U.S. RELATIONS

JULIA SUTTON
EDITOR

NOVINKA

New York

For permission to use material from this book please contact us:
Telephone 631-231-7269; Fax 631-231-8175
Web Site: http://www.novapublishers.com

LIBRARY OF CONGRESS CATALOGING-IN-PUBLICATION DATA

ISBN: 978-1-63321-253-4

Published by Nova Science Publishers, Inc. † New York

CONTENTS

PREFACE

Brazil occupies almost half of the continent of South America and is the fifth most populous country in the world. The United States has traditionally enjoyed cooperative relations with Brazil, which also is the seventh-largest economy in the world. United States administration officials have often highlighted Brazil's status as a multicultural democracy, referring to the country as a natural partner that shares values and goals with the United States. Bilateral ties have been strained from time to time, however, as the countries' occasionally divergent national interests and independent foreign policies have led to disagreements. U.S.-Brazilian relations have been particularly strained over the past year as a result of alleged National Security Agency (NSA) activities inside Brazil. Nevertheless, the countries continue to engage on issues such as trade, energy, security, racial equality, and the environment. This book discusses Brazil's political and economic situation, as well as their relations with the United States. The book also provides Brazil's human rights report for 2013; the international religious freedom report for 2012; and the investment climate statement for 2013.

Chapter 1 – The United States has traditionally enjoyed cooperative relations with Brazil, which is the seventh-largest economy in the world and is recognized by the Obama Administration's National Security Strategy as an emerging center of influence. Administration officials have often highlighted Brazil's status as a multicultural democracy, referring to the country as a natural partner that shares values and goals with the United States. Bilateral ties have been strained from time to time, however, as the countries' occasionally divergent national interests and independent foreign policies have led to disagreements. U.S.-Brazilian relations have been particularly strained over the past year as a result of alleged National Security Agency (NSA) activities inside Brazil. Nevertheless, the countries continue to engage on issues such as trade, energy, security, racial equality, and the environment.

Chapter 2 – Brazil is a constitutional, multi-party republic. In 2010 voters chose Dilma Rousseff as president in elections widely considered free and fair. Civilian authorities maintained control over security forces. Security forces committed some human rights abuses.

Chapter 3 – The constitution and other laws and policies protect religious freedom and, in practice, the government respected religious freedom. The trend in the government's respect for religious freedom did not change significantly during the year.

Chapter 4 – Foreign direct investment (FDI) into Brazil reached approximately USD 65 billion in 2012 and, according to the United Nations Conference on Trade and Development (UNCTAD) World Investment Report, Brazil is the fifth-most attractive country for FDI for the period of 2012-2014 and is consistently the largest FDI recipient in Latin America, typically receiving close to half of all South America's incoming FDI. The United States is a major foreign investor in Brazil; according to the Central Bank of Brazil, the United States had the highest stock of FDI in Brazil as of 2010, with US$104 billion. While Brazil is generally considered a friendly environment for foreign investment, complex tax and regulatory requirements exist. In most cases, these impediments apply without discrimination to both foreign and domestic firms. The Government of Brazil (GOB) generally makes no distinction between foreign and national capital in cases of direct investment.

Chapter 5 – Testimony of Thomas F. McLarty, Chairman, McLarty Associates.

Chapter 6 – Testimony of Andres R. Gluski, Chief Executive Officer, AES Corporation.

Chapter 7 – Statement of Roberto Marques, Company Group Chairman, Johnson & Johnson Consumer Companies of North America.

In: Brazil: Conditions, Issues and U.S. Relations ISBN: 978-1-63321-253-4
Editor: Julia Sutton

Chapter 1

BRAZIL: POLITICAL AND ECONOMIC SITUATION AND U.S. RELATIONS*

Peter J. Meyer

SUMMARY

The United States has traditionally enjoyed cooperative relations with Brazil, which is the seventh-largest economy in the world and is recognized by the Obama Administration's National Security Strategy as an emerging center of influence. Administration officials have often highlighted Brazil's status as a multicultural democracy, referring to the country as a natural partner that shares values and goals with the United States. Bilateral ties have been strained from time to time, however, as the countries' occasionally divergent national interests and independent foreign policies have led to disagreements. U.S.-Brazilian relations have been particularly strained over the past year as a result of alleged National Security Agency (NSA) activities inside Brazil. Nevertheless, the countries continue to engage on issues such as trade, energy, security, racial equality, and the environment.

---

* This is an edited, reformatted and augmented version of a Congressional Research Service publication RL33456, prepared for Members and Committees of Congress dated March 27, 2014.

Political and Economic Situation

Dilma Rousseff of the center-left Workers' Party was inaugurated to a four-year presidential term on January 1, 2011, inheriting a country that had benefited from 16 years of stable governance under Presidents Fernando Henrique Cardoso (1995-2002) and Luis Inácio Lula da Silva (2003-2010). She has spent much of her time in office focusing on domestic economic challenges. Brazil experienced a rapid economic expansion from 2004 to 2010, but growth began to slow in 2011. While Rousseff's efforts to stimulate domestic consumption and protect domestic industry have helped keep unemployment near record lows, economic growth has yet to accelerate, averaging 2% annually during the first three years of her term.

Rousseff has also had to contend with several political challenges. Mass demonstrations took place across Brazil in June 2013, with protesters calling for better quality public services, among other demands. Rousseff implemented some policy reforms in response to the demonstrations, but smaller-scale protests have continued to occur and could grow in size in the lead-up to Brazil hosting the World Cup in June and July 2014. The Brazilian Congress has provided additional challenges for Rousseff, with some sectors of her multiparty coalition opposing her legislative initiatives. Although Rousseff's approval rating declined significantly during 2013, it has partially recovered and stood at 41% in February 2014. National and state elections are scheduled for October 2014, and early polling suggests Rousseff is favored to win reelection.

Congressional Action

Brazil has remained a subject of interest in the 113th Congress. In June 2013, the House Committee on Ways and Means, Subcommittee on Trade, held a hearing examining the opportunities and challenges of the U.S.-Brazil trade and investment relationship. As part of the farm bill reauthorization (P.L. 113-79), Congress approved modifications to the U.S. cotton program that could help resolve a long-running trade dispute with Brazil. Congress also continued to support conservation of the Amazon Rainforest, appropriating $10.5 million for environmental programs in the Brazilian Amazon in the Consolidated Appropriations Act, 2014 (P.L. 113-76). Other measures that have been introduced in the 113th Congress include two bills designed to pressure Brazil to amend its constitution and allow the extradition of Brazilian nationals; H.R. 571 would suspend foreign assistance to Brazil, and H.R. 572 would suspend the issuance of visas to Brazilian nationals until Brazil changes its extradition policy.

POLITICAL AND ECONOMIC SITUATION

President Dilma Rousseff of the center-left Workers Party took office on January 1, 2011, and is now in the final year of her term. She inherited a country that had benefited from 16 years of capable governance under Presidents Fernando Henrique Cardoso (1995-2002) and Luis Inácio Lula da Silva (2003-2010), during whose terms Brazil made significant advances in economic stabilization and social inclusion. Rousseff has faced a series of challenges in office, however, as the Brazilian economy has slowed and citizens have taken to the streets to express a variety of frustrations. While Rousseff has won support from the Brazilian Congress for portions of her policy agenda, she occasionally has been stymied by sectors of her own multiparty coalition. Brazil continues to face considerable economic challenges as the country prepares to host the World Cup in June and July 2014 and hold national and state elections in October 2014. Nevertheless, early polling suggests that Rousseff is favored to win a second term as president.

Background

Brazil occupies almost half of the continent of South America and is the fifth most populous country in the world with 201 million citizens.[1] The country declared independence from Portugal in 1822, initially establishing a constitutional monarchy and retaining a slave-based, plantation economy. Brazil abolished slavery in 1888 and became a republic in 1889, but economic and political power remained concentrated in the hands of large rural landowners and the vast majority of Brazilians remained outside the political system. The authoritarian government of Getúlio Vargas (1930-1945) began the incorporation of the working classes but exerted strict control over labor as part of his broader push to centralize power. Vargas also increased the state's role in the economy and pursued import-substitution industrialization. Brazil enjoyed multiparty democracy between 1945 and 1964, but experienced polarization and instability as economic growth slowed, inflation increased, and populism gained strength.

The Brazilian military seized power in a 1964 coup, ushering in two decades of authoritarian rule (1964-1985). Although repressive—especially between 1969 and 1974, the Brazilian military was not as brutal as those in some other South American countries. It nominally allowed the judiciary and Congress to function during its tenure, but stifled representative democracy and civic action, carefully preserving its influence during one of the most protracted transitions to democracy to occur in Latin America. Brazil continued to pursue state-led development during most of the military era, and industrialization helped foster the transformation of Brazil into a predominantly urban society.

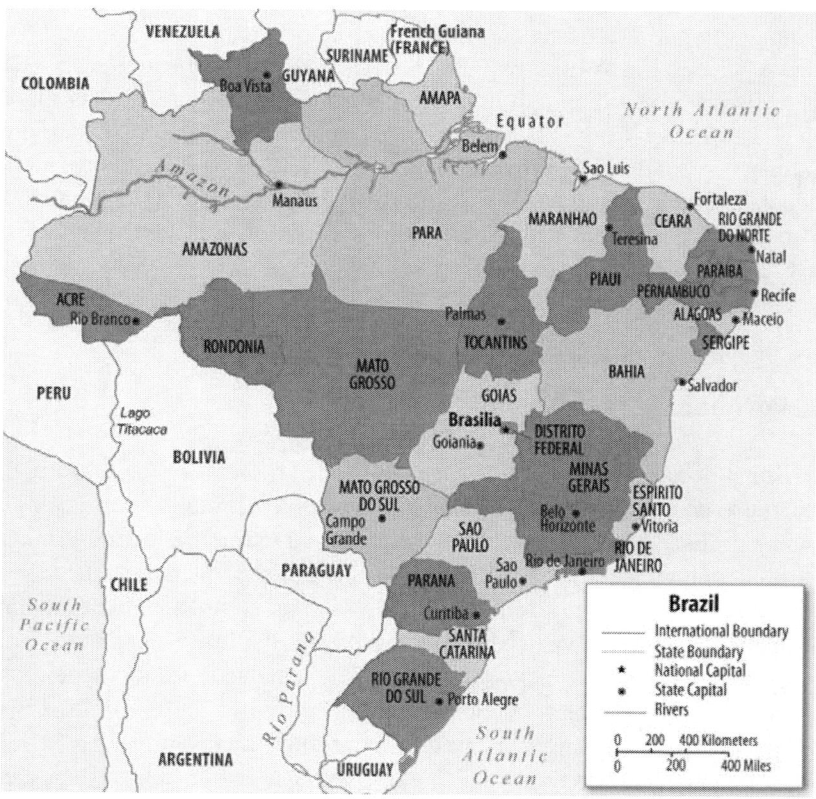

Source: Map Resources. Adapted by CRS Graphics.

Figure 1. Map of Brazil.

Brazil restored civilian rule in 1985, and a national constituent assembly, elected in 1986, promulgated a new constitution in 1988. The constitution, as amended, established a liberal democracy with a strong president, a bicameral Congress consisting of the 513-member Chamber of Deputies and the 81-member Senate, and an independent judiciary. Power is somewhat decentralized under the country's federal structure, which includes 26 states, a federal district, and some 5,570 municipalities. The reestablishment of democracy did not ensure stability, however, as Brazil experienced economic recession and political uncertainty during the first decade after the political transition. Numerous efforts to control runaway inflation failed and two elected presidents did not complete their terms; one died before taking office and the other was impeached on corruption charges.[2]

Cardoso Administration (1995-2002)

Brazil's economic and political situation began to stabilize under President Fernando Henrique Cardoso, who was elected to serve two terms between 1995 and 2002. A prominent sociologist of the centrist[3] Brazilian Social Democracy Party (*Partido da Social Democracia Brasileira*, PSDB), Cardoso's initial election in 1994 was largely the result of the success of the anti-inflation "*Real* Plan" that he implemented as finance minister under President Itamar Franco (1992-1994). The plan consisted of a new currency (the *real*) pegged to the U.S. dollar, a more restrictive monetary policy, and a severe fiscal adjustment that included a 9% reduction in federal spending and an across-the-board tax increase of 5%. Prices immediately began to stabilize, with annual inflation falling from 2,730% in 1993 to about 18% in 1995.[4] Cardoso continued the economic reform push after taking office, privatizing some state-owned enterprises and gradually opening the Brazilian economy to foreign trade and investment.

Although these policies contributed to stronger growth rates for a few years, macroeconomic stability remained elusive. Foreign investors began flooding Brazil with large capital inflows that contributed to currency appreciation and the eventual overvaluation of the *real*. Following the 1997 East Asian and 1998 Russian financial crises, concerns about Brazil's overvalued exchange rate and substantial fiscal deficits sparked a massive capital flight. Brazil was forced to adopt a floating exchange rate and the *real* lost 40% of its value.[5]

Cardoso's popularity declined as Brazil struggled with these economic challenges; however, most analysts credit him with laying the foundation for the macroeconomic stability that Brazil has experienced since he left office. In the aftermath of the 1998-1999 financial crises, Brazil adopted the three main pillars of its macroeconomic policy: a floating exchange rate, a primary budget surplus, and an inflation-targeting monetary policy. Cardoso also established a series of targeted income transfer programs designed to alleviate poverty. These economic and social policies have been maintained and built upon by subsequent administrations.

Lula Administration (2003-2010)

Luis Inácio Lula da Silva—known as Lula—was elected president of Brazil in 2002, his fourth attempt at the presidency as the candidate of the center-left[6] Workers Party (*Partido dos Trabalhadores*, PT) that he helped found as a metalworker and union leader. During his first term, Lula maintained the market-oriented economic policies associated with his predecessor. He tightly controlled expenditures, raised the primary budget surplus, and granted additional autonomy to the Central Bank. At the same time, he placed greater emphasis on reducing poverty, reorganizing and expanding some of the social programs that had been initiated under Cardoso. The most high profile program, *Bolsa Familia* ("Family Grant"), provides monthly cash transfers to poor families that ensure their children attend school and receive proper medical care. Lula's agenda stalled toward the end of his first term as several top PT officials were implicated in a vote-buying scheme. Although the scandal ultimately led to the convictions of 25 people—including Lula's former chief of staff—in 2012,[7] Lula was reelected in 2006.

After primarily focusing on maintaining economic stability during his first term, Lula established a larger role for the Brazilian state in economic development during his second term. He expanded *Bolsa Familia* and launched new social welfare programs such as *Minha Casa, Minha Vida* ("My House, My Life")—an attempt to increase formal housing for low-income Brazilians. He also continued to raise the minimum wage, which, adjusted for inflation, increased nearly 64% during his eight years in office.[8] In response to the global financial crisis, the Lula Administration implemented a series of stimulus measures designed to offset declines in global demand with increased domestic consumption. Analysts have credited the administration's timely policy response for mitigating the effects of the crisis and facilitating recovery;[9] the Brazilian economy contracted by 0.3% in 2009 before rebounding with 7.5% growth in 2010.[10] Moreover, Lula won legislative approval for a new regulatory framework that is designed to increase the state's role in the exploitation of Brazil's considerable offshore oil reserves and use the resources to fuel long-term economic and social development.

Although some observers criticized Lula for not doing more to advance certain policy reforms,[11] most give him credit for improving social inclusion in Brazil. Between 2001 and 2011, the percentage of the population living in poverty fell from 37.5% to 20.9%, and the percentage living in extreme poverty fell from 13.2% to 6.1%.[12] Income inequality was also reduced, with the Gini coefficient[13] falling from 0.64 to 0.56 during the same time period.[14] While these advances were partially the result of stronger economic growth driven by a boom in international demand for Brazilian commodities, government policy also played a role. According to a 2012 study, about 28% of the decline in income inequality in Brazil between 2001 and 2009 was attributable to increases in the minimum wage and another 12.7% of the decline was attributable to the *Bolsa Família* program.[15]

BRAZIL AT A GLANCE

Land Area: 8.5 million sq. km. (slightly smaller than the United States)

Population: 201.5 million (2014 est.)

Race/Ethnicity: White—47.7%, Brown—43.1%, Black—7.6%, Asian—1.1%, Indigenous—0.4% (Self-identification, 2010)

Religion: Catholic—65%, Evangelical Christian—22%, None—8%, Other—4% (2010)

Official Language: Portuguese

Gross Domestic Product (GDP): $2.2 trillion (2013 est.)

GDP per Capita: $10,958 (2013 est.)

Top Exports: iron ore, soy beans, oil, meat, motor vehicles and parts, machinery, and sugar (2013)

Life Expectancy at Birth: 73.2 years (2010-2015 est.)

Infant Mortality Rate: 19 per 1,000 live births (2010-2015 est.)

Adult Literacy Rate: 90.4% (2011)

Poverty Rate: 18.6% (2012)

Indigence Rate: 5.4% (2012)

Sources: Area, race/ethnicity, and religion statistics from the *Instituto Brasileiro de Geografia e Estatística* (IBGE); GDP estimates from the International Monetary Fund (IMF); trade data from Global Trade Atlas; population and social statistics from the U.N. Economic Commission for Latin America and the Caribbean (ECLAC).

Rousseff Administration (2011-Present)

Dilma Rousseff of the center-left PT was inaugurated to a four-year term in January 2011, becoming Brazil's first woman president. She had never been elected to public office prior to winning the presidency,[16] but was chosen by Lula to run as his successor. Rousseff served as minister of mines and energy from 2003 to 2005 and Lula's chief of staff from 2005 to 2010, during which time she was in charge of strategic projects such as the government's housing program, investments in infrastructure, and a new regulatory framework for developing Brazil's offshore oil reserves. Rousseff is an economist by training. She originally became involved in politics by joining underground leftist groups that fought against the military regime; Rousseff was arrested, tortured, and imprisoned for nearly three years during the authoritarian period.[17]

Although her multiparty coalition nominally holds significant majorities in both houses of the Brazilian Congress, Rousseff has struggled throughout her term to hold the ideologically diverse coalition together. Given the fragmented nature of Brazil's political system, presidents have traditionally distributed control of ministries and state enterprises to coalition partners in order to construct governing majorities. Rousseff's distribution of appointments, which heavily favors the PT over the other seven parties with representation in the 39-member cabinet, has upset some sectors of the coalition. Her dismissal of six cabinet ministers accused of corruption during her first year in office and periodic efforts to more tightly control government expenditures have exacerbated these intra-coalition divisions. In Brazil's 513-seat Chamber of Deputies, for example, the number of deputies supporting the Rousseff Administration on at least 90% of votes fell from 306 (60%) in 2011 to 123 (24%) in 2013.[18] While Rousseff has been able to win legislative support for portions of her policy agenda, she has lost key congressional votes on issues such as the distribution of oil royalties and reforms to Brazil's forest conservation law.[19]

Economic Challenges

Rousseff has spent the majority of her time in office focused on domestic economic challenges. With a gross domestic product (GDP) of $2.2 trillion,[20] Brazil is the largest economy in Latin America and the seventh-largest economy in the world. The country experienced rapid economic growth from 2004 to 2010, driven by a boom in international demand—particularly from China— for Brazilian commodities such as meat, sugar, soybeans, iron ore, and crude oil. The initial expansion was reinforced by domestic consumption from Brazil's fast-growing middle class,[21] which now accounts for a majority of the population.[22] As international commodity prices began to fall, however, economic growth slowed.

The Rousseff Administration has sought to offset the weaker international economic situation by boosting domestic consumption and protecting domestic industry. The Administration has pursued an expansionary fiscal policy, implementing a series of short-term stimulus packages. It has also adopted a new industrial policy, known as *Brasil Maior* ("Bigger Brazil"), which has included targeted tax cuts and financing through the Brazilian Development Bank (BNDES) for domestic manufacturing, stronger preferences for locally produced goods in government procurement, and restrictions on imports.[23]

While these measures have helped keep unemployment near historic lows (5.1% in February 2014),[24] economic growth has yet to recover. The Brazilian economy expanded by an average of about 2% annually from 2011 to 2013,[25] and is forecast to grow by 2.3% in 2014.[26] As a result of lower tax receipts, the Brazilian government has been forced to rely on accounting maneuvers and extraordinary revenue to meet its primary budget surplus target.[27] Moreover, these economic policies have helped push inflation to the upper edge of the government's targeted boundary (4.5% with a 2-point tolerance band), weakening citizens' purchasing power and eroding national competitiveness. In order to keep inflation under control, the Brazilian Central Bank, which previously had reduced interest rates to record lows, was forced to reverse course and adopt a tighter monetary policy.[28]

Many analysts maintain that Brazil's slower economic growth is the result of structural constraints such as "infrastructure deficiencies, high labor costs and low skill levels, a high tax burden and an onerous tax system, excessive administrative burdens, shallow credit markets, and barriers to international trade."[29] They argue that the Brazilian government should address these constraints and thereby improve productivity and boost investment, rather than continuing to try to stimulate consumption.[30] It appears as though the Rousseff Administration recognizes these constraints on growth. Among other measures, it has cut taxes and encouraged private investment in the country's overburdened infrastructure by tendering concessions to build and operate roads, railways, ports, and airports. Significant challenges remain, however, as Brazil is ranked 116th out of 189 countries in the World Banks's 2014 "Ease of Doing Business" index,[31] and gross domestic investment stands at 18.4% of GDP[32]—well below the 22%-23% of GDP that economists estimate is necessary to sustain higher economic growth.[33]

Mass Demonstrations

Mass demonstrations took place across Brazil in June 2013, and smaller protests have continued to take place periodically since then. The protests began on June 6, 2013, when about 2,000 people took to the streets of São Paulo to oppose an increase in bus fares. The crowds started to grow as Brazilians shocked by the heavy-handed police response joined in subsequent demonstrations. The situation then rapidly evolved as Brazilians began to air a broader array of grievances and news of the demonstrations was relayed through social media. At the peak of the demonstrations on June 20, 2013, an estimated 1.2 million people protested in 80 cities across Brazil.[34]

While the protesters voiced a wide range of complaints, the underlying cause of the demonstrations appears to be the government's failure to meet citizens' rising expectations. Some 40 million Brazilians have joined the middle class since 2003,[35] and many that have left poverty behind expect further improvements in their living standards. Public education, health, and transportation services are generally perceived to be low quality, however, and the slowing economy and rising cost of living have reinforced the precarious position of the new middle class. Moreover, inequality remains high by international standards despite a significant reduction over the past decade; the top 10% of Brazilians receive over 46% of all income—more than the bottom 80% of Brazilians combined.[36]

Although there continues to be broad support for Brazil's development model, which includes relatively high taxes (36.3% of GDP in 2012)[37] and an active role for the government in the economy,[38] many Brazilians believe public funds are being squandered through corruption and unnecessary expenditures. Some 200 federal legislators are reportedly facing criminal charges,[39] and, until recently, several legislators that had been convicted in high-profile corruption cases were allowed to keep their seats in Congress. The Confederations Cup soccer tournament that Brazil hosted in June 2013 as a prelude to the 2014 World Cup served as a useful backdrop for protesters seeking to highlight the divergence between the priorities of average citizens, who demand better public services, and Brazilian politicians, who are investing about $11.2 billion (R$25.6 billion)[40] to upgrade soccer stadiums and related infrastructure. Over the course of June 2013, the percentage of Brazilians rating the Rousseff Administration as "good" or "excellent" fell 27 points to 30%.[41] Politicians from other parties and at other levels of government saw similar declines, reflecting citizens' general discontent with the Brazilian political class.

The demonstrations appear to have caught Brazilian politicians off-guard.[42] Prior to the protests, President Rousseff enjoyed high approval ratings, and many in the ruling coalition assumed that Brazilians would continue to reward them politically for Brazil's decade-long rise in living standards. According to some analysts, however, it is precisely because Brazilians enjoy more economic security that they have been able to focus on broader quality of life and good governance issues.[43] Moreover, while some labor unions and social movements have close ties to, and regularly consult with, the PT and other Brazilian political parties, the protests reportedly have been fueled by youth without strong connections to the political system.[44]

In an attempt to regain the initiative, Rousseff called on Brazilian policy makers to adopt a variety of policy changes—some of which she had previously proposed—to address the protesters' demands. Her five so-called "pacts" related to fiscal responsibility, political reform, healthcare, public transportation, and education.[45] While some of Rousseff's initiatives have moved forward, others have not. Her political reform proposal found little support in the Brazilian Congress, but small-scale electoral changes and several anti-corruption and transparency measures have been enacted. The Brazilian Congress also adopted a measure to dedicate 75% of the funds generated by oil royalties to education and 25% to health care. For its part, the Rousseff Administration has increased expenditures for urban transportation projects, and created a program known as *Mais Médicos* ("More Doctors") that has brought nearly 14,000 (mainly Cuban) doctors to Brazil to work in underserved communities.[46]

Although some Brazilians have continued to protest, the demonstrations have been less frequent and smaller in scale since June 2013. The protests also appear to have lost some public support as a result of so-called "Black Bloc" demonstrators that have engaged in confrontations with police and vandalism. Between June 2013 and February 2014, the percentage of Brazilians supporting the protests fell from 81% to 52% and the percentage opposed to the protests increased from 15% to 42%.[47] Nevertheless, large-scale demonstrations could reemerge in the lead-up to the World Cup, which is scheduled to be played in Brazil between June 12 and July 13, 2014.

2014 Elections

Brazil is scheduled to hold presidential, legislative, and state office elections on October 5, 2014. President Rousseff is running for reelection as the PT's candidate and is currently attempting to solidify alliances with the rest of the parties in her ruling coalition. The principal opposition candidates appear to be Aécio Neves, a Senator from the state of Minas Gerais and the candidate of the PSDB, and Eduardo Campos, the governor of the state of Pernambuco and the candidate of the center-left Brazilian Socialist Party (*Partido Socialista Brasileiro*, PSB). Campos has forged an alliance with Marina Silva, who served as an environment minister in the Lula Administration and won 19% of the presidential vote in 2009. While the PSDB has led the political opposition since the PT first took power in 2003, the PSB was a member of the ruling coalition until September 2013. Neves and Campos have adopted similar campaign rhetoric, promising to maintain the successful social policies of the PT while increasing government efficiency, strengthening the economy, reducing crime, and improving the quality of public services.[48]

Early polling suggests that Rousseff is favored to win reelection. A February 2014 poll found that when asked to choose between the top three contenders, 47% of Brazilians would vote for Rousseff, 17% would vote for Neves, and 12% would vote for Campos. Nevertheless, there are some indications that the race could tighten. Rousseff's approval rating has only partially recovered since its precipitous drop in June 2013 and currently stands at 41%. Likewise, 67% of Brazilians say they would prefer that the next president take different actions than those of President Rousseff. Rousseff also currently benefits from higher name recognition, which will likely change over the course of the campaign. While Rousseff is known to all Brazilians, 24% have never heard of Neves and 45% have never heard of Campos.[49] If no candidate wins an absolute majority, a runoff election would be scheduled for October 26, 2014.

U.S.-Brazil Relations

The United States and Brazil have traditionally enjoyed cooperative relations. The Obama Administration's National Security Strategy recognizes Brazil as an emerging center of influence and asserts that the U.S. government welcomes Brazil's leadership to "pursue progress on bilateral, hemispheric, and global issues."[50] To this end, the countries have at least 20 active bilateral dialogues, which serve as vehicles for policy coordination on issues of mutual concern.[51] State Department officials maintain that the United States and Brazil are "natural partners" with "shared values and increasingly converging goals."[52] Through the Obama Administration's 100,000 Strong in the Americas initiative and Brazil's Science without Borders program, for example, both countries are seeking to create new academic and research partnerships and increase educational exchanges among U.S. and Brazilian students.

Nevertheless, bilateral ties have been strained from time to time as the countries' occasionally divergent national interests and independent foreign policies have led to disagreements. Several long-running disputes relate to trade, where Brazil has pushed the United States to reduce protections for U.S. agriculture and the United States has pushed Brazil to reduce protections for Brazilian industry (see "Commercial Relations"). Other disagreements have arisen as Brazil has taken on a larger role in international affairs. In 2010 and 2011, for example, Brazil used its temporary seat on the U.N. Security Council to advocate engagement with internationally isolated regimes like Iran, Libya, and Syria. While the United States and Brazil generally agreed on desired outcomes in these countries, Brazil's long-standing commitment to the peaceful resolution of conflicts and its aversion to the use of military force (or economic sanctions, which it views as a prelude to the use of force) led it to approach the issues much differently than the United States.

Bilateral relations have been particularly strained over the past year as the press has reported on alleged National Security Agency (NSA) activities in Brazil. The reports, which indicated that the NSA had spied on President Rousseff and the state-owned oil company *Petróleo Brasileiro S.A.* (Petrobras) in addition to engaging in broader electronic surveillance, led Brazil to indefinitely postpone a state visit to Washington that Rousseff was scheduled to make in October 2013. They also appear to have influenced Brazil's decision to award a $4.5 billion fighter jet procurement deal to Sweden's Saab AB over Boeing (see "Defense"). At the September 2013 U.N. General Assembly, Rousseff denounced alleged NSA activities as a breach of international law and a threat to democratic governance, stating, "I fought against authoritarianism and censorship, and I cannot but defend, in an uncompromising fashion, the right to privacy of individuals and the sovereignty of my country. In the absence of the right to privacy, there can be no true freedom of expression and opinion, and therefore no effective democracy." She also asserted that "friendly governments and societies that seek to build a true strategic partnership ... cannot allow recurring illegal actions to take place as if they were normal. They are unacceptable."[53]

U.S. Foreign Assistance and Trilateral Development Initiatives

As a middle-income country, Brazil does not receive large amounts of U.S. assistance. The United States provided Brazil with $25.5 million in FY2011, $19 million in FY2012, and $15.2 million in FY2013. The Obama Administration estimates that $13.9 million will be provided to Brazil in FY2014 and has requested $3.4 million for Brazil in FY2015 (see **Table 1**). The majority of the assistance provided in recent years has supported conservation programs in the Brazilian Amazon (see "Amazon Conservation"). The FY2015 request is significantly lower than the FY2014 estimate as a result of the Administration not requesting additional funds for these environmental programs in Brazil. The United States has also provided Brazil with security assistance, much of which has focused on counternarcotics and military capacity building efforts (see "Security Cooperation").

Table 1. U.S. Assistance to Brazil: FY2010-FY2015
In thousands of U.S. dollars

Account	FY 2010	FY 2011	FY 2012	FY 2013	FY 2014 (estimate)	FY 2015 (request)
State Department and USAID, Subtotal	**25,099**	**23,321**	**18,038**	**15,185**	**13,865**	**3,365**
DA	16,789	15,000	12,800	11,462	12,500	2,000
GHP-State	1,300	1,300	1,300	881	500	500
GHP-USAID	5,000	4,990	0	0	0	0
INCLE	1,000	1,000	3,000	2,000	0	0
NADR	400	400	300	270	240	240
IMET	610	631	638	572	625	625
DOD, Subtotal[a]	**1,928**	**2,167**	**919**	**NA**	**NA**	**NA**
1004	583	1,012	557	NA	NA	NA
2249c	0	127	247	NA	NA	NA
2561	1,345	1,028	115	NA	NA	NA
Total	**27,027**	**25,488**	**18,957**	**15,185**	**13,865**	**3,365**

Sources: U.S. Department of State, *Congressional Budget Justifications for Foreign Operations, Fiscal Years 2012, 2013, 2014, and 2015*; U.S. Department of Defense, *Reports to Congress on Foreign-Assistance Related Programs, Fiscal Years 2010, 2011, and 2012.*

Notes: DA=Development Assistance; GHP=Global Health Programs; INCLE=International Narcotics Control and Law Enforcement; NADR=Nonproliferation Anti-terrorism, Demining, and Related programs;

IMET=International Military Education and Training; 1004=DOD counternarcotics aid; 2249c=DOD counterterrorism education and training; and 2561=DOD humanitarian aid.

a. DOD assistance data for FY2013, FY2014, and FY2015 are not yet available.

Most U.S. assistance is provided through the State Department and U.S. Agency for International Development (USAID), and is funded through annual Department of State, Foreign Operations, and Related Programs appropriations measures.A small portion of U.S. assistance for Brazil is provided through the Department of Defense (DOD), and is funded through annual DOD appropriations measures.

In recent years, USAID has begun working with Brazil's development agency, the Brazilian Cooperation Agency (*Agência Brasileria de Cooperação*, ABC), in third countries. Under these so-called trilateral development initiatives, the United States and Brazil share expertise and funding in order to accomplish common goals.[54] The Administration's FY2014 budget request included funding to strengthen ABC's capacity and implement jointly funded food security projects in countries such as Haiti, Honduras, and Mozambique. It also included funding designed to foster collaboration between the Centers for Disease Control and Prevention (CDC) and the Brazilian Ministry of Health in order to combat HIV/AIDS in Brazil and Lusophone Africa.[55]

A measure introduced in the 113th Congress, H.R. 571 (T. Ryan), would suspend foreign assistance to Brazil until the country amends its constitution to allow the extradition of Brazilian nationals. The bill, which was prompted by the case of a Brazilian woman who allegedly killed her American husband before fleeing to Brazil, has yet to advance.

Commercial Relations

Trade policy has often been a contentious issue in U.S.-Brazilian relations. Over the past two decades, Brazil's trade policy has prioritized regional integration through the Common Market of the South (Mercosur)[56] and multilateral negotiations at the World Trade Organization (WTO).[57] Brazil is the industrial hub of Mercosur, which was established in 1991 and also includes Argentina, Paraguay, Uruguay, and Venezuela. While the bloc was created with the intention of incrementally advancing toward full economic integration, only a limited customs union has been achieved thus far. The group has also been plagued by internal disputes and frequent rule changes. Instead of serving as a platform for insertion into the global economy as originally envisioned, Mercosur has evolved into a more protectionist arrangement, shielding its members from external competition. Beginning in the 1990s, the United States sought to incorporate Mercosur and other sub-regional trade blocs into a hemisphere-wide Free Trade Area of the Americas (FTAA).[58] The initiative was effectively killed in 2005, however, when the United States was unable to persuade Brazil and the other members of Mercosur to continue the negotiations.

At the WTO, Brazil has played a key role in the Doha Round[59] of multilateral trade negotiations that began in 2001. It has led the G-20 group of developing nations in insisting that developed countries reduce agricultural tariffs and subsidies. Brazil has also resisted calls by the United States and other developed countries for increased access to developing nations' industrial and services sectors. In 2013, Brazil's widely respected diplomat and trade representative Roberto Azevêdo was appointed Director General of the WTO. He has sought to revive the Doha Round, successfully negotiating a small-scale agreement on trade facilitation measures in December 2013. Negotiations on more sensitive issues like agriculture reportedly remain stalled.[60]

Some Brazilian analysts have argued that the international trading system is undergoing a significant transformation and that Brazil should reconsider its current trade policy.[61] They maintain that large-scale agreements like the Trans-Pacific Partnership (TPP) and the Transatlantic Trade and Investment Partnership (TTIP)[62] could establish new and more comprehensive rules for trade and investment. By setting new global standards, the agreements could effectively bypass the current round of WTO negotiations and threaten Brazil's ability to shape the international trading system. The agreements could also place Brazilian companies at a competitive disadvantage and threaten the global market share of Brazilian exports. In order to remain relevant and take advantage of changing opportunities, these analysts argue that Brazil should conclude trade negotiations with the European Union (EU) and consider pursuing a trade agreement with the United States. While major shifts in trade policy appear to be unlikely in the near term, Brazil has already placed renewed emphasis on concluding an agreement between Mercosur and the EU.[63] Further policy shifts may depend on how the TPP and TTIP negotiations advance and economic conditions in Brazil.

Bilateral Trade and Investment

Despite these differences in trade policy and the lack of a free trade agreement, U.S.-Brazil trade has grown considerably over the past decade (see **Figure 2**). Whereas total U.S. merchandise trade with the world increased 68% between 2004 and 2013, U.S.-Brazil merchandise trade increased 105% to $71.7 billion during the same time period. U.S. goods exports to Brazil increased 218% to $44.1 billion and U.S. goods imports from Brazil increased 30% to $27.6 billion. As a result of the relatively faster growth of U.S. exports compared to imports (which declined significantly in the aftermath of the financial crisis), the United States has run a trade surplus in goods with Brazil since 2008. In 2013, the surplus was valued at $16.6 billion.[64] Top U.S. goods exports to Brazil included heavy and electric machinery, refined oil products, and civilian aircraft and parts. Top U.S. goods imports from Brazil included crude oil, iron and steel, machinery, civilian aircraft, ethanol, and coffee. In 2013, Brazil was the United States' ninth-largest trading partner, and the United States was Brazil's second-largest trading partner, behind China.[65]

U.S.-Brazil services trade has grown even more quickly than merchandise trade, increasing by 356% between 2004 and 2012 (the most recent year for which data are available). In 2012, total trade in services amounted to $30.7 billion. The United States continued to run a substantial trade surplus, valued at $17 billion, as U.S. services exports to Brazil totaled $23.9 billion and U.S. services imports from Brazil totaled $6.9 billion. Travel, telecommunications, and royalties and license fees were the top categories of U.S. services exports to Brazil while business, professional, and technical services was the top category of U.S. services imports from Brazil.[66]

Brazil has traditionally benefited from the Generalized System of Preferences (GSP), which provides non-reciprocal, duty-free tariff treatment to certain products imported from designated developing countries. Legal authorization for the GSP program expired on July 31, 2013, and Congress has yet to renew it.[67] In 2012, the last full year that the GSP was in effect, Brazil was the third-largest beneficiary of the program. The country's duty free imports to the United States under the GSP program were valued at $2.3 billion, equivalent to about 7% of all U.S. imports from Brazil in 2012.[68] Some observers have questioned the inclusion of Brazil and other upper-middle-income countries in the GSP; the European Union removed such countries from its GSP program as of 2014.[69]

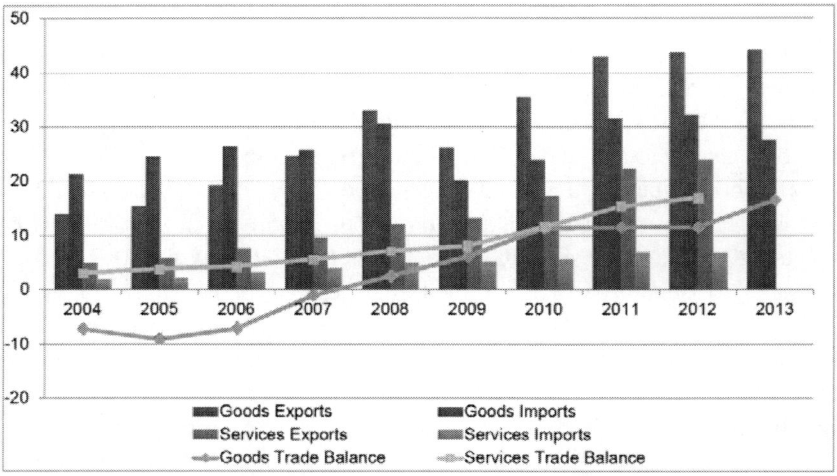

Source: CRS presentation of U.S. Department of Commerce Data.
Notes: Services trade data are not yet available for 2013.

Figure 2. U.S. Trade with Brazil: 2004-2013. In billions of U.S. dollars.

Foreign direct investment (FDI) between the United States and Brazil currently flows mostly in one direction, towards Brazil. As of 2012 (the most recent year for which data are available), the accumulated stock of U.S. FDI in Brazil was $79.4 billion, with significant investments in manufacturing and finance, among other sectors. Brazilian FDI in the United States has increased considerably over the past decade, but remains low by comparison. In 2012, the stock of Brazilian FDI in the United States totaled $3.6 billion.[70]

Cotton Dispute[71]

For more than a decade, Brazil and the United States have been involved in a dispute over U.S. government support for cotton farmers. In 2002, Brazil went to the WTO to challenge several provisions of the U.S. cotton program. AWTO dispute settlement panel ruled in Brazil's favor in 2004, finding that certain U.S. agricultural support payments and export guarantees were inconsistent with its WTO commitments. Although Congress modified agricultural support programs in 2005, a WTO compliance panel ruled in 2007 that the U.S. actions were insufficient. Following a ruling from a WTO arbitration panel, Brazil announced in March 2010 that it intended to impose retaliatory measures against the United States worth $829 million. This included $591 million in higher tariffs on a range of U.S. products and $239 million through suspension of certain intellectual property rights obligations.

The United States reached a temporary agreement with Brazil in June 2010 to avoid the WTO-sanctioned retaliatory measures. Under the agreement, the United States pledged to make some short-term changes to its export credit guarantees and provide the Brazil Cotton Institute with $147 million annually for a fund to assist Brazilian cotton farmers with technical assistance, marketing, and market research. In exchange, Brazil agreed to temporarily suspend its retaliation with the intention of reaching a permanent agreement with the United States after Congress had an opportunity to adjust the subsidy program in the farm bill reauthorization.[72]

The U.S. government stopped complying with the temporary agreement in 2013, however, making only a portion of the required monthly payment in September 2013 and then stopping payments altogether as of October 2013. Secretary of Agriculture Tom Vilsack reportedly asserted that the partial payment was required by budget sequestration and that he had no authority to continue making payments once the farm bill expired at the end of September.[73] The suspension of payments led the Brazilian government to once again explore retaliatory measures.[74]

Congress passed a new farm bill (P.L. 113-79) that President Obama signed into law on February 7, 2014. The conference report accompanying the act (H.Rept. 113-333) states that the legislation includes several substantive changes to U.S. cotton support programs and the export credit guarantee program in order to resolve the dispute with Brazil. Nevertheless, Brazil's Foreign Trade Board (*Câmara de Comércio Exterior*, CAMEX) maintains that the new farm bill contains elements that will continue to distort the international cotton market, and it has authorized the Brazilian government to request a WTO panel to assess whether the farm bill brings the United States into compliance with previous rulings.[75] The Brazilian government has reportedly decided not to immediately request such a panel and instead enter into negotiations with the United States in hope of achieving a mutually agreeable resolution.[76]

Energy Ties

Energy has been another important area of U.S.-Brazilian cooperation in recent years. Brazil is widely regarded as a world leader in energy policy for successfully reducing its reliance on foreign oil through the development of alternative energy resources and increased domestic production. In addition to being the world's second-largest producer of ethanol (after the United States), Brazil generates 80% of its electricity through hydropower.[77] Brazil also has discovered large offshore oil deposits that have the potential to turn the country into a major oil and gas producer and an important source of energy for the United States. To facilitate greater cooperation in the development of safe, secure, and affordable energy, President Obama and President Rousseff launched a Strategic Energy Dialogue in March 2011.

Biofuels

In response to sharp increases in global oil prices in the 1970s, the Brazilian government began a national program to promote the production and consumption of sugarcane ethanol. Today, most cars in Brazil are capable of running on pure ethanol, which is available at nearly every fueling station, or gasoline, which is required to include a 20%-25% ethanol blend.[78] Ethanol's share of the Brazilian light-duty fuel market reportedly declined from 50% in 2009 to 30% in 2012, however, as the Brazilian government held down gasoline prices as part of its efforts to control inflation.[79] Government policy and international sugar prices that have provided incentives for sugarcane processors to produce sugar rather than ethanol have contributed to lower levels of investment and production in the ethanol industry. In 2012, Brazil produced 405,000 barrels per day of ethanol, which was more than it produced in 2011 but less than it produced 2010.[80] The Brazilian government has sought to provide some relief to the ethanol industry by raising gasoline prices, increasing the ethanol blend requirement from 20% to 25%, and reducing taxes on ethanol. Nevertheless, some analysts maintain that the lack of transparency and certainty regarding how gasoline prices are determined are likely to continue to discourage investment in the industry.[81]

In 2007, the United States and Brazil, the world's two largest ethanol-producing and consuming countries, signed a memorandum of understanding to promote greater cooperation on ethanol and other biofuels. The agreement involves (1) technology sharing between the United States and Brazil; (2) feasibility studies and technical assistance to build domestic biofuels industries in third countries; and (3) multilateral efforts to advance the global development of biofuels.[82]

Since then, the United States and Brazil have moved forward on all three facets of the agreement. Bilaterally, the U.S. and Brazilian governments are attempting to improve methods for modeling the sustainability of biofuels, including their effects on greenhouse gas emissions and land use, and exchanging information on how to maximize fuel economy in flex-fuel vehicles. They are also coordinating efforts to develop sustainable aviation biofuels. At the same time, the U.S. and Brazilian governments are working together in third countries, and have provided joint technical assistance designed to strengthen policy frameworks, implement blending laws, and develop domestic production capabilities in the Dominican Republic, El Salvador, Guatemala, Haiti, Honduras, Jamaica, and Senegal. Multilaterally, the United States and Brazil are working with other members of the Global Bioenergy Partnership (GBEP) to promote the sustainable production and use of modern bioenergy.[83]

In addition to these efforts, Brazil and the United States have taken steps to liberalize trade in ethanol. In December 2011, the Brazilian government issued a resolution to extend its duty-free treatment of imported ethanol until December 31, 2015.[84] Similarly, the U.S. Congress allowed a 54-cent-per-gallon duty on imported ethanol to expire at the end of 2011. Prior to its expiration, the duty served as a significant barrier to direct imports of Brazilian ethanol in most years.[85] Total bilateral ethanol trade has actually declined since then, however, falling from 33,000 barrels per day in 2011 to 19,000 barrels per day in 2013. This decline is the result of lower U.S. exports to Brazil, as imports from Brazil have increased from 7,000 barrels per day to 16,000 barrels per day during the same time period. In 2013, U.S. imports from Brazil were equivalent to about 1.8% of total U.S. ethanol consumption.[86]

Oil

Since 2007, Brazil has discovered substantial new offshore oil fields that have the potential to turn the country into one of the top five oil and gas producers in the world[87] and an important source of energy for the United States. The new discoveries are so-called "pre-salt" reserves, located beneath layers of rock and salt more than 18,000 feet below the ocean surface. Some energy analysts have estimated that the total recoverable reserves of pre-salt oil and natural gas may exceed 50 billion barrels of oil equivalent.[88] Brazil's proven oil reserves stood at 15.3 billion barrels at the end of 2012, accounting for slightly less than 1% of global reserves.[89] Nearly 94% of Brazil's proven reserves are located offshore.[90]

In December 2010, the Brazilian Congress approved a new regulatory framework for developing the approximately 70% of pre-salt reserves that had not already been auctioned off.[91] The new framework increased the role of the Brazilian government and is designed to ensure that the country's oil reserves are used to fuel long-term economic and social development. Among other provisions, the framework establishes state-owned Petróleo Brasileiro S.A. (Petrobras) as the sole operator for all new offshore projects; replaces the existing concessionary model with a production sharing regime; guarantees Petrobras a minimum 30% stake in all new joint ventures; creates a new public company—Petrosal—to manage the development of the offshore reserves; increases local content requirements; and creates a new social fund overseen by the Brazilian Congress to direct offshore revenues toward four key areas: education, infrastructure, science and technology, and poverty reduction.[92] The Brazilian Congress continued to debate a new law regarding the distribution of oil royalties until March 2013.[93]

The delay in approving the new regulatory framework and royalty distribution law prevented Brazil's National Agency of Petroleum, Natural Gas, and Biofuels (*Agência Nacional do Petróleo, Gás Natural e Biocombustíveis*, ANP) from auctioning new concessions for nearly five years. As a result, oil production did not increase as quickly as originally predicted and actually slightly declined between 2011 and 2012 to 2.1 million barrels per day.[94] Even so, the Brazilian government received record revenues from the oil industry in 2012 that amounted to about $14 billion (R$31.8 billion).[95]

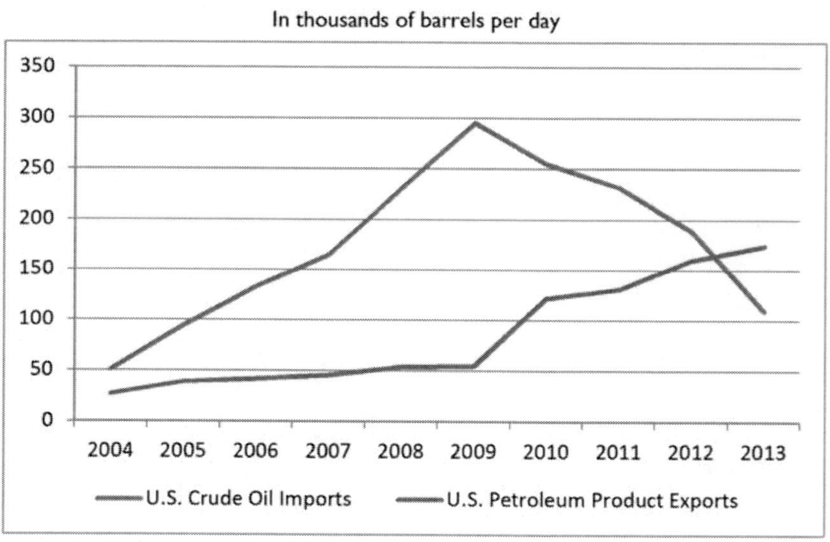

Source: CRS presentation of U.S. Energy Information Administration (EIA) data.

Figure 3. U.S. Oil Trade with Brazil: 2004-2013.

The ANP held its first auction of pre-salt concessions under the new regulatory framework in October 2013. While the ANP reportedly had expected more than 40 companies to participate, only 11 companies signed up for the auction, and a consortium of five companies (Petrobras, Royal Dutch Shell, Total, China National Petroleum Corporation, and China National Offshore Oil Corporation) was the sole bidder.[96] The Brazilian government declared the auction a success, but some energy analysts maintain that the country will need to modify the new regulatory framework prior to auctioning other concessions in order to attract the investment necessary to develop its reserves and accelerate production.[97]

U.S.-Brazilian oil trade has expanded significantly over the past decade (see **Figure 3**). U.S. crude oil imports from Brazil grew rapidly from 51,000 barrels per day in 2004 to 295,000 barrels per day in 2009. They have declined since then, however, as U.S. consumption has fallen and U.S. domestic production has increased. In 2013, the United States imported 109,000 barrels per day of crude oil from Brazil, which was equivalent to about 1.4% of total U.S. crude imports. U.S. exports of refined products to Brazil have also grown quickly, increasing 544% from 27,000 barrels per day in 2004 to 174,000 barrels per day in 2013. As a result, U.S. refined product exports to Brazil exceeded U.S. crude imports from Brazil for the first time in at least a decade in 2013.[98] Brazil has been forced to increasingly rely on imports as its consumption has grown more quickly than its production and refinery capacity. Some energy analysts expect this trend to continue until at least 2017, when two new Brazilian refineries are scheduled to begin operations.[99]

Security Cooperation

Although U.S.-Brazilian cooperation on security issues has traditionally been limited, law enforcement and military ties have increased in recent years. Areas of coordination include counternarcotics, counterterrorism, and defense.

Counternarcotics

While Brazil is not a major drug-producing country, it is the world's second-largest consumer of cocaine hydrochloride and likely the world's largest consumer of cocaine-base products. It also serves as a transit point for illicit drugs destined for Europe.[100] Security analysts contend that organized crime in Brazil has increased in scope and scale over the past decade as the drug trade has expanded. Some of the country's large, well-organized, and heavily armed criminal groups, such as the Red Command (*Comando Vermelho*, CV) and the First Capital Command (*Primeiro Comando da Capital*, PCC), have reportedly begun to operate transnationally, eliminating intermediaries in order to control cross-border trafficking.[101]

In recognition of these challenges, Brazil has taken several steps to improve its antidrug efforts. In 2004, it implemented an air bridge denial program, which authorizes lethal force for air interdiction, and in 2006, Brazil passed an anti-drug law that prohibits and penalizes the cultivation and trafficking of illicit drugs. Brazil has also sought to improve security along the 15,719 kilometer border that it shares with 10 nations, including the region's cocaine producers— Bolivia, Colombia, and Peru. Under its Strategic Border Plan, introduced in June 2011, the Brazilian government has reportedly deployed inter-agency resources, including unmanned aerial vehicles (UAVs), to monitor illicit activity in high-risk locations along its borders and in the remote Amazon region. It has also signed agreements and carried out joint operations with neighboring countries.[102] In 2013, Brazilian authorities reportedly seized 35.7 metric tons of cocaine and 220.8 metric tons of marijuana.[103]

In 2008, the U.S. and Brazilian governments signed a memorandum of understanding designed to enhance the capacity of Brazilian authorities to combat drug trafficking and reduce domestic drug demand. To these ends, the United States provided support to a canine unit and special investigation units within the Brazilian Federal Police, and provided support to non-governmental organizations that work with addicts and their families in 2013.[104] U.S. counternarcotics assistance to Brazil amounted to $2 million in FY2011, $3.5 million in FY2012, and $1.9 million in FY2013.[105] The Obama Administration did not request any counternarcotics assistance for Brazil in FY2014 or FY2015.[106]

Counterterrorism[107]

The Tri-Border Area (TBA) of Argentina, Brazil, and Paraguay has long been used for arms smuggling, money laundering, and other illicit purposes. According to the State Department's *Country Reports on Terrorism*, there are no known operational cells of al Qaeda or Hezbollah-related groups in the Western Hemisphere; however, the United States remains concerned that proceeds from legal and illegal goods flowing through the TBA could potentially be diverted to support terrorist groups.[108] For example, in December 2010, the U.S. Treasury Department sanctioned Hezbollah's chief representative in South America, Bilal Mohsen Wehbe, for transferring funds collected in Brazil to Hezbollah in Lebanon. According to the Treasury Department, Wehbe and an associate raised more than $500,000 from Lebanese businessmen in the TBA following the 2006 conflict between Israel and Hezbollah. Wehbe also reportedly had overseen Hezbollah's counterintelligence activity in the TBA and had worked for the office of Iranian Supreme Leader Ayatollah Ali Khamene'i.[109]

The U.S. government has worked with Brazil to address concerns about the TBA and strengthen the country's counterterrorism capabilities. The countries of the TBA and the United States created the "3+1 Group on Tri-Border Area Security" in 2002, and the group built a Joint Intelligence Center to combat trans-border criminal organizations in 2007. Within Brazil, the United States has supported efforts to implement the Container Security Initiative (CSI) at the port of Santos, and has sought to strengthen Brazil's capacity to secure its borders and conduct terrorism-related investigations. U.S. authorities are currently assisting Brazil with major event security management as it prepares to host the 2014 World Cup and 2016 Summer Olympic Games.[110]

The State Department's *Country Reports on Terrorism* for 2012 recognized the Brazilian government's continued support for counterterrorism-related activities, including investigating potential terrorism financing and document forgery networks.[111] However, Brazil has yet to adopt legislation to make terrorism and terrorism financing autonomous offenses. Like many other Latin American nations, Brazil has been reluctant to adopt specific antiterrorism legislation as a result of the difficulty of defining terrorism in a way that does not include the actions of social movements and other groups whose actions of political dissent were condemned as terrorism by repressive military regimes in the past. Despite these challenges, some Brazilian legislators have renewed their efforts to enact an anti-terrorism law, maintaining that Brazil needs to strengthen its legal framework in advance of the upcoming major sporting events.[112]

Defense

According to General John F. Kelly, Commander of U.S. Southern Command, challenges in broader bilateral relations have affected U.S.-Brazilian defense ties, but military-to-military cooperation at the operational and tactical levels remains strong.[113] The U.S. and Brazilian militaries have worked together closely in Haiti, where Brazil commands the U.N. Stabilization Mission (MINUSTAH). Joint efforts in the aftermath of Haiti's January 2010 earthquake were the largest combined operations of U.S. and

Brazilian military forces since World War II. Other areas of military-to-military cooperation include information exchanges, combined military training, and joint military exercises. In April 2010, the U.S. and Brazilian governments signed a Defense Cooperation Agreement designed to promote cooperation in areas such as research and development, technology security, and acquisition of defense products and services. This was followed by a General Security of Military Information Agreement, signed in November 2010, which is designed to facilitate the sharing of classified defense and military information.[114] Both agreements still need to be approved by the Brazilian Congress. Additional coordination takes place through a presidential-level Defense Cooperation Dialogue, which President Obama and President Rousseff launched in April 2012.

As noted above, the United States provides International Military Education and Training (IMET) aid to Brazil. The assistance is designed to strengthen military-to-military relationships, increase the professionalization of Brazilian forces, and enhance Brazil's capacity to assume a larger role in peacekeeping operations and in combating terrorism. IMET assistance amounted to $631,000 in FY2011, $638,000 in FY2012, and $572,000 in FY2013. Brazil is receiving an estimated $625,000 in IMET in FY2014, and the Administration has requested $625,000 in IMET assistance for Brazil in FY2015.[115]

Two defense procurement deals have received considerable attention in recent years. In February 2013, the U.S. Air Force awarded a $427 million contract for light air support aircraft and associated maintenance and training to Brazil's Embraer S.A. and its U.S.-based partner, Sierra Nevada Corp. Under the contract, Embraer will provide 20 *A-29 Super Tucano* aircraft to the Afghan military for advanced flight training, surveillance, close air support, and air interdiction missions.[116] The U.S. Air Force had originally awarded the contract to Embraer in December 2011, but the order was cancelled after U.S.-based Hawker Beechcraft challenged the procurement process.

Some observers assumed that the U.S. contract with Embraer increased the likelihood that Brazil would award a contract for 36 new fighter jets to Boeing. Brazil awarded the $4.5 billion contract to Sweden's Saab AB in December 2013, however, choosing the Gripen NG over Boeing's F/A-18 Super Hornet. While the decision appears to have been at least partially a reaction to alleged NSA surveillance activities inside Brazil, there were also other considerations.[117] The Brazilian Air Force announced its preference for the Gripen in January 2010, reportedly citing its lower purchase and maintenance costs and the ability to transfer more technology to Brazil.[118]

Given Brazil's current economic challenges and the fact that some Brazilian officials were already wary of relying on U.S. hardware as a result of past experiences in which the U.S. government blocked sales of Brazilian arms containing U.S. technology,[119] the NSA allegations may have been enough to push Boeing out of the running.

Promotion of Racial Equality

Brazil has experienced significant improvements in economic and social conditions over the past decade; however, considerable socioeconomic disparities between races persist. While Afro-Brazilians comprise about half of the Brazilian population,[120] they account for less than 25% of Brazilians that have completed post-secondary degrees and 17% of Brazilians that have completed graduate degrees.[121] In 2010, the median income of Afro-Brazilians was 64% of the median income of white Brazilians.[122] Even after controlling for education, occupation, and location, white Brazilians reportedly receive higher wages than Afro-Brazilians.[123] Moreover, Afro-Brazilians are disproportionately the victims of Brazil's high levels of crime and violence. In 2010, the homicide rate for Afro-Brazilians was 36.5 per 100,000—nearly two and a half times the rate of other Brazilians.[124]

In order to reduce racial disparities, the Brazilian government has enacted a series of antidiscrimination and affirmative action measures. Brazil became the first Latin American country to endorse racial quotas in government service in 2002, and became the first country in the world to establish a special secretariat with a ministerial rank to manage racial equity promotion policies in 2003. In 2010, Brazil enacted the Statute of Racial Equality. Among other provisions, the law offers tax incentives for businesses that undertake racial inclusion, calls on the government to adopt affirmative action programs, and reaffirms that African and Afro-Brazilian history should be taught in all elementary and middle schools. In 2012, Brazil adopted a law that requires federal universities to reserve half of their admissions spots for students who are Afro-Brazilian, indigenous, or graduates of public high schools (which tend to serve the poorest students). The law gradually increases the admissions spots required to be reserved from 12.5% in 2013 to 50% in 2016, with half of the reserved spots set aside for low income students of all races with the highest grades and the other half divided in accordance with the racial makeup of each state.[125] Most recently, President Rousseff has proposed reserving 20% of jobs in the federal government for Afro-Brazilians.[126] Although race-based affirmative action policies have been rather controversial among some sectors of the Brazilian population,[127] they have been upheld as constitutional by the Brazilian Supreme Court.

In March 2008, Brazil and the United States signed an agreement known as the United States-Brazil Joint Action Plan to Eliminate Racial and Ethnic Discrimination and Promote Equality. The initiative recognizes that Brazil and the United States are multi-ethnic, multi-racial democracies, and seeks to promote equality of opportunity for the members of all racial and ethnic communities. To that end, Brazil and the United States share best practices through activities such as training programs, workshops, technical expert exchanges, scholarships, and public-private partnerships.[128] Current areas of focus include expanding access to education for students of African descent, eliminating racial health disparities, mitigating environmental impacts in communities of African descent, addressing challenges in criminal justice systems, and guaranteeing equal access to economic opportunities.[129] H.Rept. 113-185, which is considered part of the explanatory statement accompanying the Consolidated Appropriations Act, 2014 (P.L. 113-76), recognizes the work being done under the U.S.-Brazil Joint Action Plan to Eliminate Racial and Ethnic Discrimination and Promote Equality, and states that the legislation includes funds to continue the initiative in FY2014.

Amazon Conservation

The Amazon Basin is estimated to span more than 6.8 million square kilometers. It produces about 20% of the world's fresh water discharge and contains the largest remaining rainforest on Earth.[130] In addition to supporting significant biological diversity, the Amazon Rainforest is a global sink for carbon emissions and an important asset in the mitigation of climate change. The forest biomass is estimated to hold about 100 billion tons of carbon, which is equivalent to more than 10 years of global fossil fuel emissions.[131]

Although the Amazon Basin is shared by seven nations,[132] 69% of it lies within Brazil.[133] The Brazilian Amazon was largely undeveloped until the 1960s, when the military government began subsidizing the settlement and development of the region as a matter of national security. Partially as a result of these incentives, the human population grew from 6 million in 1960 to 25 million in 2010. Forest cover in the Brazilian Amazon has declined to about 80% of its original area as a result of settlements, roads, logging, farming, and other activities in the region.[134]

Recognizing that continued destruction of the Amazon Rainforest is damaging to Brazil's global image and could threaten energy generation and agricultural production in the future,[135] the Brazilian government has implemented a series of policies designed to slow deforestation. From 2004 to 2011, for example, Brazil increased the size of its nature reserves by 500,000 square kilometers. Likewise, the Brazilian government adopted a plan to reduce the rate of Amazon deforestation by 80%—based on the 1996-2005 average—to 3,925 square kilometers per year by 2020. To meet this target, the Brazilian government is increasing surveillance, replanting forest, and financing sustainable development projects.[136] Brazil appears to be on track to achieve its goal, as annual deforestation has fallen from 27,772 square kilometers in 2004 to 5,843 square kilometers in 2013 (see **Figure 4**).[137] There is considerable debate, however, as to whether these decreases are the result of government policies or changing economic circumstances, such as lower commodity prices. According to a 2012 study, about half of the reduction in deforestation in the Brazilian Amazon between 2005 and 2009 was attributable to the Brazilian government's conservation policies.[138]

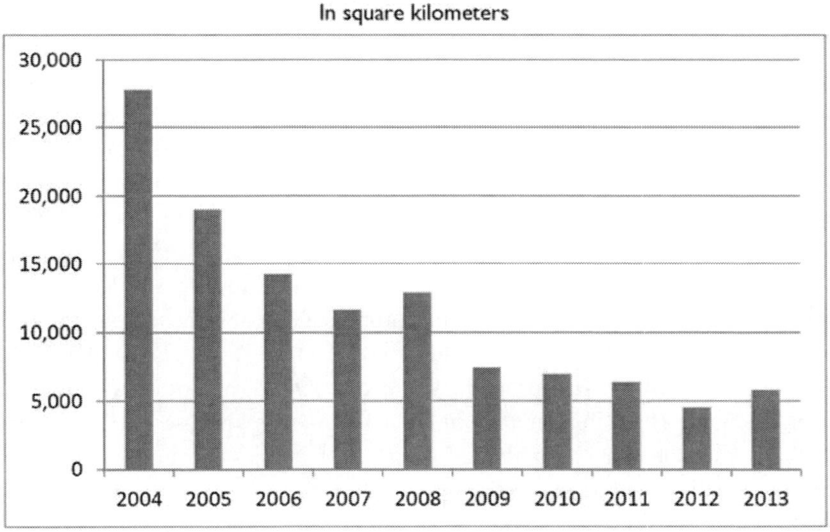

Source: CRS presentation of data from the Brazilian government's *Instituto Nacional de Pesquisas Espaciais* (INPE).

Figure 4. Deforestation in the Brazilian Amazon: 2004-2013.

Despite recent progress, Brazil's deforestation rate increased by nearly 28% between 2012 and 2013—a development that some analysts have attributed to government policy changes. In 2011, President Rousseff signed a law transferring responsibility for environmental oversight of non-federal lands from Brazil's federal environmental protection agency to local officials. While the federal government maintains that local officials are better placed to manage such resources, critics argue that local authorities lack the necessary finances and are more susceptible to intimidation and corruption.[139] Many environmentalists are also concerned about changes to Brazil's forest code—a law that requires rural landowners to set aside 20%-80% of their land for natural vegetation. The Brazilian Congress approved a major overhaul of the code in 2012. Although President Rousseff vetoed some of the most controversial provisions, the final version reportedly relaxed conservation requirements for environmentally sensitive areas like river banks, reduced reforestation requirements for land that had already been deforested, and decreased the total amount of forest that must be preserved.[140] Supporters of the reform assert that it was necessary in order to bring farmers into compliance with the law, and argue that the updated forest code remains among the strictest regulations of privately owned property in the world.[141]

In recent years, the United States has provided assistance to Brazil designed to support tropical forest conservation through the promotion of sustainable land use and encouragement of environmentally friendly income generation activities for the rural poor. In FY2006, USAID initiated the Amazon Basin Conservation Initiative, which supports community groups, governments, and other organizations working throughout the Amazon Basin to conserve the forest's biodiversity. USAID provided Brazil with $11.5 million for environmental programs in FY2011, $10.8 million in FY2012, and $9.6 million in FY2013.[142] The explanatory statement[143] accompanying the Consolidated Appropriations Act, 2014 (P.L. 113-76) stipulates that $10.5 million of the funds appropriated by the act should support environmental programs in the Brazilian Amazon in FY2014. As was the case in FY2013 and FY2014, the Obama Administration has not requested any funding for environmental programs in Brazil in FY2015.[144]

In addition to providing foreign aid, the United States has signed a debt-for-nature agreement with Brazil under the Tropical Forest Conservation Act of 2008 (P.L. 105-214). According to the August 2010 agreement, the United States is reducing Brazil's debt payments by $21 million over five years. In exchange, the Brazilian government is committing those funds to activities to conserve protected areas, improve natural resource management, and develop sustainable livelihoods in endangered areas outside of the Amazon Rainforest such as the Atlantic Rainforest, Caatinga, and Cerrado ecosystems.[145]

APPENDIX. LEGISLATIVE INITIATIVES IN THE 113TH CONGRESS

P.L. 113-79 (H.R. 2642). Agricultural Act of 2014. Signed into law on February 7, 2014. Includes changes to the U.S. cotton program that could allow for a resolution to a long-standing WTO dispute with Brazil.

P.L. 113-76 (H.R. 3547). Consolidated Appropriations Act, 2014. Signed into law on January 17, 2014. The explanatory statement accompanying the act stipulates that $10.5 million of the funds appropriated should support environmental programs in the Brazilian Amazon. H.Rept. 113-185 (which accompanied H.R. 2855 and is considered part of the explanatory statement) recognizes the work being done under the U.S.-Brazil Joint Action Plan to Eliminate Racial and Ethnic Discrimination and Promote Equality, and states that the legislation includes funds to continue the initiative in FY2014.

S. 744 (Schumer). Border Security, Economic Opportunity, and Immigration Modernization Act. Agreed to in the Senate on June 27, 2013. Includes a provision that would require U.S. consular missions to explore options for expanding visa processing capacity in Brazil.

H.R. 1644 (Kind). Introduced April 18, 2013; referred to the House Committee on Agriculture. Among other provisions, would prohibit the Secretary of Agriculture from making payments to the Brazilian Cotton Institute. The payments are part of a temporary agreement between the United States and Brazil regarding the WTO cotton dispute.

H.R. 571 (T. Ryan). Karl Hoerig Foreign Aid Suspension Act. Introduced February 6, 2013; referred to the House Committee on Foreign Affairs. Would suspend U.S. assistance to Brazil until it amends its constitution to allow the extradition of Brazilian nationals.

H.R. 572 (T. Ryan). End Immunity for Brazilian Criminals Act. Introduced February 6, 2013; referred to the House Committee on the Judiciary. Would suspend the issuance of visas to Brazilians until Brazil amends its constitution to allow the extradition of Brazilian nationals.

End Notes

[1] United Nations Economic Commission for Latin America and the Caribbean (ECLAC), *Statistical Yearbook for Latin America and the Caribbean, 2013*, December 2013, p.33, http://www.eclac.cl/publicaciones/xml/5/51945/ AnuarioEstadistico2013.pdf.

[2] *Brazil: A Country Study*, ed. Rex A. Hudson, 5th ed. (Washington, DC: Library of Congress, 1998).

[3] The PSDB was founded as a center-left party by dissidents from the social democratic wing of the Party of the Brazilian Democratic Movement (*Partido do Movimento Democrático Brasileiro*, PMDB). It has moved to the right, however, since implementing market-oriented economic reforms during the Cardoso Administration. Timothy J. Power and Cesar Zucco Jr., "Estimating Ideology of Brazilian Legislative Parties, 1990-2005," *Latin American Research Review*, vol. 44, no. 1, 2009.

[4] CRS Report 98-987, *Brazil's Economic Reform and the Global Financial Crisis*, by J. F. Hornbeck.

[5] Ibid; Riordan Roett, "How Reform has Powered Brazil's Rise," Current History, February 2010.

[6] Although the PT was founded as a leftist party, it moved toward the ideological center upon taking office in 2002. Power and Zucco, 2009, op.cit.

[7] "Brazil Politics: Supreme Court Gives Tough Sentences in 'Mensalão' Trial," *Economist Intelligence Unit*, October 26, 2012.

[8] Cristiano Romero, "O Legado de Lula na Economia," *Valor Online* (Brazil), December 29, 2010.

[9] See, for example, International Monetary Fund (IMF), "IMF Executive Board Concludes 2010 Article IV Consultation with Brazil," August 5, 2010.

[10] IMF, *World Economic Outlook Database, October 2013*, accessed February 2014.

[11] See, for example, "Brazil's Presidential Election: Lula's Legacy," *Economist*, September 30, 2010; and Paulo Kliass, "Lula's Political Economy: Crisis and Continuity," *North American Congress on Latin America (NACLA)*, March/April 2011.

[12] ECLAC, *Statistical Yearbook for Latin America and the Caribbean, 2012*, December 2012, p.65, http://www.eclac.cl/publicaciones/xml/4/48864/AnuarioEstadistico2012_ing.pdf.

[13] The Gini coefficient is a value between zero and one, where zero represents complete equality and one represents complete inequality.

[14] ECLAC, December 2012, op.cit., p.70.

[15] Pedro H. G. Ferreira de Souza, *Poverty, Inequality and Social Policies in Brazil, 1995-2009*, U.N. Development Programme, International Policy Centre for Inclusive Growth, Working Paper Number 87, Brasilia, February 2012, p.19, http://www.ipc-undp.org/pub/IPCWorkingPaper87.pdf.

[16] Rousseff won 56% of the vote to defeat José Serra of the PSDB in a second round runoff election on October 31, 2010. The second round was necessary since Rousseff had fallen just short of an absolute majority—with 47% of the vote—in the first round election held on October 3, 2010. In the first round, she was followed by Serra at 33%, and Marina Silva, a former Lula Administration environment minister that ran for president as the candidate of the Green Party (*Partido Verde*, PV), at 19%.

[17] Presidência da República Federativa do Brasil, "Presidenta: Biografia," July 4, 2011.

[18] José Roberto de Toledo, Isadora Peron, and Rodrigo Burgarelli, "PSD e PSB Puxam Derrotas do Governo na Câmara; Núcleo Fiel a Dilma Fica 60% Menor," *O Estado de São Paulo*, January 20, 2014.

[19] Joe Leahy, "Brazil Grapples with Dysfunctional Congress; Controversy over Pastor Highlights Complexity of Dealing with a Congress Hostage to Diverse Interest Groups," *Financial Times*, April 10, 2013.

[20] IMF, *World Economic Outlook Database, October 2013*, accessed February 2014.

[21] The Brazilian government breaks the population into five income classes: A, B, C, D, and E. Those in the "C" class, who earn approximately $760-$3,280 (R$1,734-7,475) per month, are generally referred to as the "new middle class."

[22] Marcelo Cortes Neri, *Os Emergentes dos Emergentes: Reflexões Globais e Ações para a Nova Classe Média Brasileira*, Fundação Getulio Vargas, Rio de Janeiro, June 27, 2011, p.35.

[23] "Brazil: Propping Up Industry," *Economist Intelligence Unit*, August 15, 2011; Howard Schneider, "Brazil's Inward Turn Bothers U.S." *Washington Post*, December 4, 2012.

[24] Instituto Brasileiro de Geografia e Estatística (IBGE), "Unemployment Rate was 5.1% in February," March 27, 2014.

[25] IMF, *World Economic Outlook Database, October 2013*, accessed February 2014.

[26] IMF, *World Economic Outlook Update, Is the Tide Rising?*, January 21, 2014.

[27] Paulo Trevisani, "Brazil Changes Budget; Freezes Some Spending to Regain Markets' Confidence," *Wall Street Journal*, February 20, 2014.

[28] Walter Brandimarte, "Insight – Brazil's Tombini: An Inflation Hawk, Believe It or Not," *Reuters*, August 23, 2013.

[29] Organisation for Economic Co-operation and Development (OECD), *OECD Economic Surveys: Brazil*, October 2013.

[30] Ibid; "The Days of Easy Growth are Over for Now," *Latin America Monitor: Brazil,* July 2013; IMF, *Brazil: Staff Report for the 2013 Article IV Consultation*, IMF Country Report No. 13/312, Washington, DC, October 2013, http://www.imf.org/external/pubs/ft/scr/2013/cr13312.pdf.

[31] World Bank, "Ease of Doing Business in Brazil," http://www.doingbusiness.org/data/exploreeconomies/brazil.

[32] IMF, October 2013, op.cit., p.45.

[33] Joe Leahy, "Investors Worry the Dilma Model is Unravelling in Brazil," *Financial Times*, May 20, 2013.

[34] "Brazil's Stormy June: Not Turkey or Egypt," *Latin American Security & Strategic Review*, June 2013.

[35] Neri, 2011, op.cit., p.35.

[36] ECLAC, December 2013, op.cit., p.77.

[37] OECD, ECLAC, and Inter-American Center of Tax Administrations, *Revenue Statistics in Latin America, 1990-2012*, January 2014.

[38] For example, a November 2013 poll found that 67% of Brazilians think the government, rather than the private sector, should be most responsible for investing to produce economic growth. Ricardo Mendonça, "Brasileiros se Dividem sobre Impostos e Papel do Governo," *Folha de São Paulo*, December 8, 2013.

[39] Simon Romero, "Public Rage Catching Up With Brazil's Congress," *New York Times*, June 27, 2013.

[40] República Federativa do Brasil, Ministério do Esporte, "Matriz de Responsabilidades Consolidada," September 2013.

[41] "Avaliação da Presidente Dilma Rousseff," *Datafolha*, June 28, 2013.

[42] Francisco Peregil, "Las Protestas Dejan a Brasil Perplejo," *El País* (Spain), June 23, 2013; "A Direção do PT está em Pânico, Diz Historiador," *Folha de São Paulo*, June 23, 2013.

[43] Bob Moser, "Record Low Unemployment Fueling Protestor Confidence in Brazil," *MercoPress*, July 2, 2013.

[44] Fernando Rodrigues, "Movimento está Divorciado dos Políticos Tradicionais," *Folha de São Paulo*, June 18, 2013.

[45] Presidência da República Federativa do Brasil, "Discurso da Presidenta da República, Dilma Rousseff, durante Reunião com Governadores e Prefeitos de Capitais," June 24, 2013.

[46] Paulo Victor Chagas, "Cinco Pactos Foram a Resposta do Governo Federal aos Protestos de Junho," *Agência Brasil*, December 31, 2013; Johanna Nublat, "Com Nova Leva, Cubanos Serão 82% do Mais Médicos," *Folha de São Paulo*, March 6, 2014.

[47] Fabiano Maisonnave, "Aprovação à Realização da Copa é a Menor em 5 Anos," *Folha de São Paulo*, February 24, 2014.

[48] Gustavo Patu, "Críticas de Aécio e Campos ao PT são Quase Idênticas," *Folha de São Paulo*, February 9, 2014.

[49] Datafolha, *Intenção de Voto para Presidente 2014*, February 20, 2014; Fernando Rodrigues, "Dilma Para de Subir, Mas Seria Reeleita No 1° Turno," *Folha de São Paulo*, February 23, 2014.

[50] White House, *National Security Strategy*, May 2010, p. 44.

[51] U.S. Department of State, Bureau of Western Hemisphere Affairs, "U.S. Relations with Brazil," Fact Sheet, October 3, 2013.

[52] William J. Burns, Deputy Secretary of State, "Building a Deeper Partnership with Brazil," Remarks in Rio de Janeiro, Brazil, March 1, 2012.

[53] President Dilma Rousseff, *Statement by H.E. Dilma Rousseff, President of the Federative Republic of Brazil, at the Opening of the General Debate of the 68th Session of the United Nations General Assembly*, September 24, 2013.

[54] Paulo Sotero, *Shaping U.S.-Brazil Relationship after the Snowden Affair: A Conversation with Ambassador Thomas A. Shannon*, Woodrow Wilson International Center for Scholars, Brazil Institute, Special Report, Washington, DC, February 2014, http://www.wilsoncenter.org/sites/default/files/AmbassadorThomas%20Shannon%20-%20Final.pdf.

[55] U.S. State Department, *Congressional Budget Justification for Foreign Operations, Fiscal Year 2014, Annex: Regional Perspectives*, July 2, 2013, http://www.state.gov/documents/organization/208291.pdf.

[56] For background information on Mercosur, see CRS Report RL33620, *Mercosur: Evolution and Implications for U.S. Trade Policy*, by J. F. Hornbeck.

[57] João Augusto de Castro Neves, *Brazil's Slow and Uncertain Shift from Protectionism to Free Trade*, Inter-American Dialogue, Working Paper, January 2014, http://www.thedialogue.org/uploads/CastroNeves_Trade.pdf.

[58] For background information on the FTAA see CRS Report RS20864, *A Free Trade Area of the Americas: Major Policy Issues and Status of Negotiations*, by J. F. Hornbeck.

[59] For more information on the Doha Round, see CRS Report RL32060, *World Trade Organization Negotiations: The Doha Development Agenda*, by Ian F. Fergusson.

[60] "The World Trade Organization: Unaccustomed Victory," *The Economist*, December 14, 2013.

[61] See, for example, "Chances Perdidas," *Correio Braziliense*, January 2, 2014; Sonia Filgueiras, "Olhar do Planalto – Sob o Risco do Isolamento," *Brasil Econômico*, December 18, 2013; and Vera Thorstensen and Lucas Ferraz, *The Impacts of TTIP on Brazil*, Fundação Getulio Vargas, Study Sponsored by the Confederação Nacional da Industria (CNI), November 2013.

[62] For more information on these agreements, see CRS Report R42694, *The Trans-Pacific Partnership (TPP) Negotiations and Issues for Congress*, coordinated by Ian F. Fergusson; and CRS Report R43387, *Transatlantic Trade and Investment Partnership (TTIP) Negotiations*, by Shayerah Ilias Akhtar and Vivian C. Jones.

[63] Carlos Caicedo, "Brazil Keen to Speed Up EU-Mercosur Free-Trade Deal at Expense Argentina," *IHS Global Insight*, March 13, 2014.

[64] U.S. Department of Commerce data, as made available by the U.S. International Trade Commission, *Interactive Tariff and Trade DataWeb*, accessed March 2014.

[65] U.S. Department of Commerce and República Federativa do Brasil, Secretaria de Comércio Exterior (SECEX) data as made available by *Global Trade Atlas*, accessed March 2014.

[66] U.S. Department of Commerce data, as made available by the Bureau of Economic Analysis, accessed March 2014.

[67] For more information on GSP and potential congressional reauthorization of the program, see CRS Report RL33663, *Generalized System of Preferences: Background and Renewal Debate*, by Vivian C. Jones.

[68] U.S. Department of Commerce data, as made available by the U.S. International Trade Commission, *Interactive Tariff and Trade DataWeb*, accessed March 2014.

[69] European Commission, "New GSP as of 2014," December 18, 2013.

[70] U.S. Bureau of Economic Analysis, "Balance of Payments and Direct Investment Position Data," accessed March 2014.

[71] For more information on the U.S.-Brazil WTO cotton dispute, see CRS Report R43336, *Status of the WTO Brazil-U.S. Cotton Case*, by Randy Schnepf.

[72] Swell Chan, "U.S. and Brazil Reach Agreement on Cotton Dispute," *New York Times*, April 6, 2010; Ana Nicolaci da Costa, "Brazil Suspends Retaliation in U.S. Cotton Row," *Reuters*, June 17, 2010.

[73] William Mauldin, "U.S. to Stop Brazil Farm Payments; Sequester Will Stop Assistance Related to Cotton Dispute," *Wall Street Journal*, August 7, 2013.

[74] República Federativa do Brasil, Ministério do Desenvolvimento, Indústria e Comércio Exterior, Câmara de Comércio Exterior (CAMEX), *Resolução N° 105, de 18 de Dezembro de 2013.*

[75] CAMEX, "CAMEX Autoriza Abertura de Painel na OMC sobre Legislação Agrícola Norte-Americana," February 19, 2014.

[76] "Brazil Threatens Compliance Panel Over Farm Bill; Pursues Negotiations First," *Inside U.S. Trade*, February 20, 2014.

[77] U.S. Energy Information Administration (EIA), *Country Analysis Briefs: Brazil*, October 1, 2013.

[78] Ibid.

[79] Claire Casey, "Is Brazil the Energy Power of the Future (and Always Will Be)?," *Americas Quarterly*, (Summer 2013).

[80] EIA, October 2013, op.cit.

[81] Casey, 2013, op.cit.

[82] U.S. Department of State, Office of the Spokesman, "Memorandum of Understanding Between the United States and Brazil to Advance Cooperation on Biofuels," March 9, 2007, http://www.state.gov/p/wha/rls/158654.htm.

[83] White House, Office of the Press Secretary, "Fact Sheet: The U.S.-Brazil Strategic Energy Dialogue," April 9, 2012.

[84] Ministério do Desenvolvimiento, Indústria e Comércio Exterior, Câmara de Comércio Exterior (CAMEX), *Resolução N° 94, de 8 de Dezembro de 2011.*

[85] Although some Brazilian ethanol was allowed to enter the United States duty-free after being reprocessed in Caribbean Basin Initiative (CBI) countries, such imports could only account for up to 7% of the U.S. ethanol market. A 2.5% ad valorem tariff on ethanol imports to the United States remains in place permanently unless the Harmonized Tariff Schedule code is changed.

[86] EIA, "Petroleum & Other Liquids: Data," accessed March 2014.

[87] Mark S. Langevin, *Brazil's Hydrocarbon Bonanza: Can the State Manage Pre-Salt Production for National Development and Geopolitical Power?*, Brazil-Works, Discussion Paper, May 2012.

[88] EIA, October 2013, op.cit.

[89] BP, *BP Statistical Review of World Energy*, June 2013, p. 6, http://www.bp.com/content/dam/bp/pdf/statistical-review/statistical_review_of_world_energy_2013.pdf.

[90] Agência Nacional do Petróleo, Gás Natural e Biocombustíveis (ANP), *Oil, Natural Gas and Biofuels Statistical Yearbook 2013*, 2013, p. 26.

[91] Langevin, 2012, op.cit.

[92] "Brazil Congress Passes Oil Industry Overhaul," *Reuters*, December 1, 2010; "The Impact of Pre-Salt: A Long-Term Perspective," *Oxford Analytica*, May 2010.

[93] The royalty distribution law has not yet gone into effect as it is being challenged in Brazil's Supreme Court.

[94] BP, June 2013, op.cit., p.8.

[95] ANP, 2013, op.cit.

[96] "Weak Libra Interest Rounds Out a Rough Week for Brazil's Rousseff," *Latin News Daily Report*, September 20, 2013; "Brazil's Oil Revolution Gets Off to a Slippery Start," *Latin News Daily Report*, October 22, 2013.

[97] Matthew Cowley and Paulo Trevisani, "Brazil Seen Having to Alter Oil Rules," *Wall Street Journal*, October 22, 2013.

[98] EIA, "Petroleum & Other Liquids: Data," accessed March 2014.

[99] Jeb Blount, "Analysis: Petrobras Fuel Woes Make Brazil Dependent on U.S., India," *Reuters*, January 22, 2014.

[100] U.S. Department of State, Bureau of International Narcotics and Law Enforcement Affairs, *International Narcotics Control Strategy Report (INCSR), Volume I: Drug and Chemical Control*, March 2014, http://www.state.gov/j/inl/rls/ nrcrpt/2014/vol1/222851.htm.

[101] Robert Muggah and Guztavo Diniz, *Securing the Border: Brazil's "South America First" Approach to Transnational Organized Crime*, Igarapé Institute, Strategic Paper 5, October 2013, http://pt.igarape.org.br/wp-content/uploads/2013/10/SP_05_EN_Securing-the-border_7th_oct.pdf.

[102] U.S. Department of State, Bureau of International Narcotics and Law Enforcement Affairs, *International Narcotics Control Strategy Report (INCSR), Volume I: Drug and Chemical Control,* March 7, 2012, http://www.state.gov/j/inl/rls/nrcrpt/2012/vol1/184098. htm#Brazil; "Hermes 450: O Vigilante Das Fronteiras Brasileiras," *Terra* (Brazil), August 25, 2011; "Brazil-Region: Flying Start for the New 'Border Strategy'," *Latin American Security & Strategic Review*, July 2011.

[103] *INCSR*, 2014, op.cit.

[104] Ibid.

[105] U.S. Department of State, USAID, and U.S. Department of Defense data as presented by the *Foreign Assistance Dashboard*, accessed March 2014.

[106] U.S. State Department, *Congressional Budget Justification for Foreign Operations, Fiscal Year* 2014, May 17, 2013, and *Congressional Budget Justification, Department of State, Foreign Operations, and Related Programs, Fiscal Year 2015*, March 4, 2014.

[107] For more information on terrorism concerns in Latin America, see CRS Report RS21049, *Latin America: Terrorism Issues*, by Mark P. Sullivan and June S. Beittel.

[108] U.S. Department of State, Office of the Coordinator for Counterterrorism, *Country Reports on Terrorism 2012*, May 30, 2013, http://www.state.gov/j/ct/rls/crt/2012/209984.htm.

[109] U.S. Department of the Treasury, "Treasury Targets Hizballah Financial Network," Press Release, December 9, 2010.

[110] *Country Reports on Terrorism 2012*, May 2013, op.cit.

[111] Ibid.

[112] Fernanda Odilla and Gabriela Guerreiro, "Lei Antiterrorismo Pode Dar Pena de Até 40 Anos a Manifestantes," *Folha de São Paulo*, February 12, 2014; Paloma Rodrigues, "Após Morte de Cinegrafista, Senado Tenta Acelerar 'Lei Antiterror'," *CartaCapital*, February 11, 2014.

[113] General John F. Kelly, Commander, United States Southern Command, *Posture Statement before the 113th Congress House Armed Services Committee*, February 26, 2014, p. 21, http://www.southcom.mil/newsroom/Documents/2014_SOUTHCOM_Posture_Statement_ HASC_FINAL_PDF.pdf.

[114] U.S. Department of Defense, Office of the Secretary of Defense, "Fact Sheet: U.S.-Brazil Defense Cooperation," March 14, 2011.

[115] U.S. Department of State, *Congressional Budget Justifications for Foreign Operations, Fiscal Years 2013, 2014, and 2015*, available at http://www.state.gov/f/releases/iab/index.htm.

[116] "Brazilian Firm to Provide Aircraft to Afghan Air Force," *American Forces Press Service*, February 27, 2013.

[117] Alfonso Soto and Brian Winter, "Saab Wins Brazil Jet Deal after NSA Spying Sours Boeing Bid," *Reuters*, December 18, 2013.

[118] Raymond Colitt, "Brazil Air Force Prefers Swedish Jets – Report," *Reuters*, January 5, 2010.

[119] In 2006, for example, the United States prevented Brazil from selling 24 *Super Tucano* light attack planes to Venezuela.

[120] According to Brazil's 2010 census, 43.1% of Brazilians self-identify as *parda* ("brown") and 7.6% self-identify as *preta* ("black"). IBGE, *Censo Demográfico 2010*, November 2011.

[121] Tatiana Dias Silva and Fernanda Lira Goes, *Igualdade Racial no Brasil: Reflexões no Ano Internacional dos Afrodescendentes*, Instituto de Pesquisa Econômica Aplicada (IPEA), Rio de Janeiro, 2013, p. 20.

[122] IBGE, 2011, op.cit.

[123] Dias & Goes, 2013, op.cit., p.21.

[124] Daniel R. C. Cerqueira and Rodrigo Leandro de Moura, *Vidas Perdidas e Racismo no Brasil*, IPEA, Nota Técnica N° 10, Brasília, November 2013, p. 6.

[125] Simon Romero, "Brazil Enacts Affirmative Action Law for Universities," *New York Times*, August 30, 2012; "Rousseff Decrees Affirmative Action," *Latin News Daily Report*, October 16, 2012.

[126] Tatiana Dias Silva and Josenilton Marques da Silva, *Reserva de Vagas para Negros em Concursos Públicos: Uma Análise a partir do Projeto de Lei 6.738/2013*, (IPEA), Nota Técnica N° 17, Brasília, February 2014.

[127] See, for example, Diogo Schelp, "Queremos Dividir o Brasil como na Foto?" *Veja*, September 2, 2009; and Julia Carvalho, "O Grande Erro das Cotas," *Veja*, August 29, 2012.

[128] U.S. Department of State, Bureau of Western Hemisphere Affairs, "U.S.-Brazil Joint Action Plan Promotes Racial and Ethnic Equality," April 11, 2012.

[129] U.S. Department of State, Office of the Spokesperson, "Steering Group Meeting of the U.S.-Brazil Joint Action Plan to Eliminate Racial and Ethnic Discrimination and Promote Equality," Media Note, July 17, 2013.

[130] United Nations Environment Programme (UNEP), *Global International Waters Assessment: Amazon Basin*, GIWA Regional Assessment 40b, Kalmar, Sweden, 2004, http://www.unep.org/dewa/giwa/areas/reports/r40b/ giwa_regional_assessment_40b.pdf.

[131] Eric A. Davidson et al., "The Amazon Basin in Transition," *Nature*, vol. 481 (January 19, 2012), p. 321.

[132] The seven nations that share the Amazon Basin are Brazil, Bolivia, Colombia, Ecuador, Guyana, Peru, and Venezuela. The Amazon Rainforest extends beyond the Amazon Basin into Suriname and French Guiana.

[133] UNEP, 2004, op.cit.

[134] Davidson et al., 2012, op.cit., p.321.

[135] See, for example, Fabiana Frayssinet, "Climate Change-Brazil: Farmers 'Have Good Reason to Worry'," *Inter Press Service*, September 21, 2011; and "Amazonian Deforestation May Cut Rainfall by a Fifth: Study," *Agence France Presse*, September 5, 2012.

[136] República Federativa do Brasil, Ministério do Meio Ambiente, *Plano de Ação para Prevenção e Controle do Desmatamento na Amazônia Legal (PPCDAm): 3ª Fase (2012-2015)*, Brasília, June 2013.

[137] República Federativa do Brasil, Ministério da Ciência, Tecnologia e Inovação, Instituto Nacional de Pesquisas Espaciais (INPE), *Projeto PRODES, Monitoramento da Floresta Amazônica Brasileira por Satélite*, accessed March 2013.

[138] Juliano Assunção, Clarissa C. e Grandour, and Rudi Rocha, *Deforestation Slowdown in the Legal Amazon: Prices or Policies*, Climate Policy Initiative, Working Paper, Rio de Janeiro, February 6, 2012, http://climatepolicyinitiative.org/wp-content/uploads/2012/03/Deforestation-Prices-or-Policies-Working-Paper.pdf.

[139] Paulo Prada, "Special Report: Brazil Backslides on Protecting the Amazon," *Reuters*, August 3, 2012.

[140] "Brazil President Makes Final Changes to Forestry Law," *Agence France Presse*, October 18, 2012.

[141] Reese Ewing, "Interview-Brazil Land Use Bill to Make Forests Profitable," *Reuters*, June 1, 2011; Kátia Abreu, "Código Florestal e a Busca da Perfeição," *Folha de São Paulo*, September 29, 2012.

[142] USAID data, as presented by the *Foreign Assistance Dashboard*, accessed March 2014.

[143] The joint explanatory statement is available from the House Committee on Rules at http://rules.house.gov/bill/113/ hr-3547-sa.

[144] U.S. Department of State, *Congressional Budget Justification, Department of State, Foreign Operations, and Related Programs, Fiscal Year 2015*, March 4, 2014.

[145] U.S. Department of State, Office of the Spokesman, "Debt-for-Nature Agreement to Conserve Brazil's Tropical Forests," August 12, 2010. For more information on the Tropical Forest Conservation Act, see CRS Report RL31286, *Debt-for-Nature Initiatives and the Tropical Forest Conservation Act: Status and Implementation*, by Pervaze A. Sheikh.

In: Brazil: Conditions, Issues and U.S. Relations ISBN: 978-1-63321-253-4
Editor: Julia Sutton

Chapter 2

BRAZIL 2013 HUMAN RIGHTS REPORT*

U.S. Department of State; Bureau of Democracy, Human Rights and Labor

EXECUTIVE SUMMARY

Brazil is a constitutional, multi-party republic. In 2010 voters chose Dilma Rousseff as president in elections widely considered free and fair. Civilian authorities maintained control over security forces. Security forces committed some human rights abuses.

The most significant human rights abuses included poor and at times life-threatening conditions in some prisons, sex trafficking of children and adolescents, forced labor, and exploitative working conditions.

Other human rights problems included excessive force and unlawful killings by state police; excessive force, beatings, abuse, and torture of detainees and inmates by police and prison security forces; prolonged pretrial detention and inordinate delays of trials; judicial censorship of media; government corruption; violence and discrimination against women; violence against children, including sexual abuse; social conflict between indigenous communities and private landowners that occasionally led to violence; discrimination against indigenous persons and minorities; violence and social

* This is an edited, reformatted and augmented version of a report released by the U.S. Department of State; Bureau of Democracy, Human Rights and Labor, dated February 2014.

discrimination against lesbian, gay, bisexual, and transgender (LGBT) persons; insufficient enforcement of labor laws; and child labor in the informal sector.

The government continued to prosecute officials who committed abuses; however, an inefficient judicial process delayed justice for victims and perpetrators of human rights violations.

Section 1. Respect for the Integrity of the Person, Including Freedom from

a. Arbitrary or Unlawful Deprivation of Life

The federal government or its agents did not commit politically motivated killings, but unlawful killings by state police occurred. In some cases police employed indiscriminate force. In a few instances, civilians died during large-scale police operations, mainly in the favelas (poor neighborhoods or shantytowns). Credible reports indicated that state police officials continued to be involved in revenge killings and intimidation of witnesses who testified against police officials. Police often were responsible for investigating charges of torture and excessive force carried out by fellow officers.

In Rio de Janeiro there were reports that both on- and off-duty police employed indiscriminate use of force. These acts often occurred in the city's approximately 763 favelas, where an estimated 1.4 million persons lived, according to the 2010 census by the Brazilian Institute of Geography and Statistics (IBGE). The Rio de Janeiro Public Security Institute, a state government entity, reported that from January to July police killed 197 civilians in "acts of resistance" (similar to resisting arrest) in Rio de Janeiro state, compared with 263 during the same period in 2012. Most of these deaths occurred while police were conducting operations against drug-trafficking gangs operating in Rio's poor communities. A disproportionate number of the victims were Afro-Brazilian under 25 years of age. Nongovernmental organizations (NGOs) in Rio de Janeiro questioned whether all of the 197 victims had truly resisted arrest, contending that police continued to depend on repressive methods.

On June 24, the Special Police Operations Battalion entered the New Holland favela within Rio de Janeiro in pursuit of criminals. The operation resulted in a gunfight that left 10 dead, including at least two residents who were not implicated in criminal activity and Sergeant Ednelson do Santos.

In another case Rio de Janeiro resident Amarildo de Souza went missing after officers from the Police Pacification Unit (UPP) operating in the Rocinha favela brought him in for questioning on July 14. Family members claimed the police were responsible for his disappearance; other Rocinha residents alleged that police offered them money in exchange for false testimony casting suspicion on drug traffickers. In September the Public Ministry charged 10 UPP police officers, including commanding officer Major Edson Santos, with torture, murder, and hiding the body of de Souza.

The Sao Paulo State Secretariat for Public Security reported that state military police killed 239 civilians from January to June, compared with 251 in the same period in 2012.

In April a court sentenced police officer Carlos Adilio Maciel Santos from the Seventh Military Police Battalion in Rio de Janeiro to 19 years and six months in prison for the 2011 killing of Judge Patricia Lourival Acioli. Four other military police officers were already tried, convicted, and sentenced while the six remaining defendants continued to await trial dates.

b. Disappearance

There were no reports of politically motivated disappearances.

c. Torture and Other Cruel, Inhuman, or Degrading Treatment or Punishment

Although the constitution prohibits such treatment and provides severe legal penalties for its use, reports of torture and other cruel treatment by police and prison guards occurred. In July the UN Subcommittee on Prevention of Torture expressed concern about the use of torture by security forces.

A Pernambuco state judge released Paraiba state military policeman Gleson de Campos Pereira on bail under partial house arrest to await sentencing from a state court. Campos Pereira was arrested in Pernambuco on charges of torture during the apprehension of four persons suspected of robbery in 2011.

As of November the National Justice Council (CNJ) had not updated its website with the results of its most recent 2012 and 2013 prison inspections. Previous reports indicated evidence of torture and cruel, inhumane, and degrading treatment in prisons.

Prison and Detention Center Conditions

Conditions in many prisons were poor and sometimes life threatening, but many states made efforts to improve conditions. Abuse by prison guards continued to occur at many facilities. Poor working conditions and low pay for prison guards encouraged corruption.

Physical Conditions: Overcrowding was a problem. According to a Ministry of Justice report, as of December 2012 there were 548,003 prisoners – 512,964 male and 35,039 female prisoners – incarcerated nationwide in a system designed for approximately 310,690. An estimated 36 percent of all detainees were awaiting trial. Of the total prison population, approximately 34,000 were under 18 years of age.

The states of Rio de Janeiro and Sao Paulo and the Federal District provided separate prison facilities for women; elsewhere, according to the Catholic Church's Penitentiary Commission, women occasionally were held with men in some facilities.

Federal prisons and state detention centers in the state of Sao Paulo faced severe overcrowding. Government data showed that correctional facilities in the state were 87 percent over capacity and nearly one-third more crowded than in the previous four years.

Frequently prisoners who committed petty crimes were held with murderers and other violent criminals. Authorities attempted to hold pretrial detainees separately from convicted prisoners, but lack of space often required holding convicted criminals in pretrial detention facilities. Many prisons, including in the Federal District, attempted to separate prisoners based on crimes committed to separate violent offenders from nonviolent ones and to keep convicted drug traffickers in a wing apart from the rest of the prison population.

The law stipulates that juveniles should not be held together with adults in jails, but this was not always respected. Multiple sources reported adolescents jailed with adults in poor and crowded conditions. Insufficient capacity in juvenile detention centers was widespread.

In Piaui state alone, inmates killed seven fellow prisoners in the first half of the year. The CNJ considered Anibal Bruno, located in Pernambuco state, the worst prison in the country. Despite receiving 26 million reais ($11.2 million) in public funds for improvements and the construction of new facilities, it continued to face severe overcrowding, with 5,234 prisoners in a facility designed for 1,448.

Prisoners had access to potable water, but sanitary conditions were often inadequate and facilitated the spread of disease. HIV and tuberculosis prevalence rates in prisons were far higher than rates for the general population.

Administration: Recordkeeping on prisoners was adequate. The National Justice Council set up an online database during the year to monitor prisoners' cases and time served, but this system did not always function properly.

Authorities used alternatives to sentencing for nonviolent offenders. Individuals sentenced to less than eight years in prison had the option to serve in "semi-open" conditions, whereby the individual could work during the day and sleep at the prison facility at night. The CNJ found, however, that thousands of prisoners sentenced to semi-open facilities, served their sentences in "closed," or high- security, facilities.

According to Sao Paulo authorities, one-third of prisoners eligible to work did so. Prisoners and detainees had access to visitors. Human rights observers reported that some visitors complained of screening procedures that at times included invasive and unsanitary physical exams. Prisoners could observe their religious practices and could submit complaints to judicial authorities. State-level ombudsman offices and the federal Secretariat of Human Rights (SDH) officials also monitored prison and detention center conditions.

Independent Monitoring: The government permitted monitoring by independent nongovernmental observers, including the International Committee of the Red Cross. During the year the CNJ conducted prison inspections in 14 states, although it did not make its reports publicly available.

Improvements: After a four-year review of more than 413,000 prisoners' cases, in 2012 the CNJ announced it had freed more than 36,000 prisoners who had been unlawfully remanded to detention and recommended the transfer of more than 72,000 prisoners to reduced security conditions in accordance with federal sentencing guidelines.

In September the state of Paraiba announced that its three main prisons would feature exclusive wings for LGBT prisoners. The Secretariat for Prison Administration adopted the measure to diminish sexual and physical violence against gay and transgender inmates.

Alagoas state finished construction of a new prison in Craibas, designed to include dedicated cells for disabled inmates.

d. Arbitrary Arrest or Detention

The law prohibits arbitrary arrest and detention and limits arrests to those caught in the act of committing a crime or arrested by order of a judicial authority; however, police at times did not respect this prohibition.

Role of the Police and Security Apparatus

The Federal Police, operating under the Ministry of Justice, is a small, primarily investigative entity and plays a minor role in routine law enforcement. Most police forces fall under the control of the states, where they are divided into two distinct units: the civil police, performing an investigative role, and the military police, charged with maintaining law and order.

Despite its name, the military police do not report to the Ministry of Defense. The law mandates that special police courts exercise jurisdiction over state military police except those charged with "willful crimes against life," primarily homicide. The police often were responsible for investigating charges of torture and excessive force carried out by fellow officers, although independent investigations increased. Delays in the special military police courts allowed many cases to expire due to statutes of limitations.

The Brazilian Association of Investigative Journalism reported that police tactics, including excessive force, rubber bullets, and tear gas, resulted in injuries to hundreds of individuals, including at least 15 journalists during June 13protests in Sao Paulo.

According to the Rio de Janeiro State Secretariat for Public Security, human rights courses were a mandatory component of training for entry-level military police officers. UPP officers for the favela pacification program received additional human rights training. Under the pacification program, the Rio de Janeiro State Secretariat for Public Security inaugurated six new UPPs during the year, for a total of 34. As of September, 8,592 UPP officers were responsible for patrolling approximately 226 favela areas in Rio de Janeiro state.

In Rio de Janeiro's favelas, so-called militia groups, composed of off-duty and former law enforcement officers, often took policing into their own hands. Many militia groups intimidated residents and conducted illegal activities such as extorting protection money and providing pirated utility services. Human rights observers believed that militia groups controlled up to one-half of Rio's favelas.

Former Alagoas police officer Edgelson Ribeiro Guimaraes and 10 other members of an illegal militia group, arrested in mid-2011 for committing murders in the states of Pernambuco and Alagoas, were freed on bail awaiting trial, but Ribeiro Guimaraes was arrested again on August 22 for alleged involvement in a robbery in Pernambuco. He was later cleared of the robbery charges but remained in prison awaiting trial for homicide.

Arrest Procedures and Treatment of Detainees

With the exception of arrests of suspects caught in the act of committing a crime, arrests must be made with a warrant issued by a judicial official. Officials must advise suspects of their rights at the time of arrest or before taking them into custody for interrogation. The law prohibits use of force during an arrest unless the suspect attempts to escape or resists arrest. According to human rights observers, some detainees complained of physical abuse by police officers while being taken into custody.

Authorities generally respected the constitutional right to a prompt judicial determination of the legality of detention. Detainees were informed promptly of the charges against them. The law permits provisional detention for up to five days under specified conditions during an investigation, but a judge may extend this period. A judge may also order temporary detention for an additional five days for processing. Preventive detention for an initial period of 15 days is permitted if police suspect that a detainee may leave the area.

The law does not provide for a maximum period for pretrial detention, which is decided on a case-by-case basis. Time in detention before trial is subtracted from the sentence.

Defendants arrested in the act of committing a crime must be charged within 30 days of arrest. Other defendants must be charged within 45 days, although this period may be extended. The backlog in the courts often resulted in extending the period for charging defendants.

Bail was available for most crimes, and defendants facing charges for all but the most serious crimes have the right to a bail hearing. Prison authorities generally allowed detainees prompt access to a lawyer. Indigent detainees have the right to a lawyer provided by the state. Detainees also were allowed prompt access to family members.

Pretrial Detention: Despite constitutional protections, CNJ inspectors found that authorities improperly or illegally detained thousands of individuals. Approximately 200,000 of the country's 550,000 prisoners were in pretrial detention status. In some cases individuals waited years for a court to rule on the merits of their case.

e. Denial of Fair Public Trial

The constitution provides for an independent judiciary, and the government generally respected judicial independence. Freedom House stated that corruption within the judiciary, especially at the local and state level, remained a serious concern, and the judiciary was often subject to outside influences.

Although the law requires that trials be held within a set time, the nationwide backlog in state and federal cases frequently led courts to dismiss old cases unheard. There were millions of backlogged cases at the state, federal, and appellate courts. For defendants and victims, it could take years for the system to hold criminal perpetrators accountable for their actions.

Trial Procedures

The right to a fair public trial as provided by law was generally respected. NGOs reported that in some rural regions – especially in cases involving land rights activists – the perception existed that police, prosecutors, and the judiciary were more susceptible to external influences, including fear of reprisals. Investigations, prosecutions, and trials in these cases often were delayed. After an arrest a judge reviews the case, determines whether it should proceed, and assigns the case to a state prosecutor, who decides whether to issue an indictment. Juries hear cases involving capital crimes; judges try those accused of lesser crimes. Defendants enjoy a presumption of innocence and have the right to be promptly informed of charges, to access government-held evidence and confront and question adverse witnesses, to present their own witnesses and evidence, and to appeal verdicts. Defendants generally had adequate time and facilities to prepare a defense.

While the law provides for the right to counsel, the Ministry of Justice stated that many prisoners could not afford an attorney. The court must furnish a public defender or private attorney at public expense in such cases, but staffing deficits persisted in all states.

Political Prisoners and Detainees

There were no reports of political prisoners or detainees.

Civil Judicial Procedures and Remedies

Citizens can bring lawsuits before the courts for human rights violations. While the justice system provides for an independent civil judiciary, courts were overburdened with backlogs and sometimes subject to corruption, political influence, and indirect intimidation. Cases involving violations of an individual's human rights may be submitted through petitions by individuals or organizations to the Inter-American Commission on Human Rights (IACHR), which in turn may submit the case to the Inter-American Court of Human Rights.

f. Arbitrary Interference with Privacy, Family, Home, or Correspondence

Although the law and constitution prohibit such actions, NGOs reported that police occasionally conducted searches without warrants. Human rights groups, other NGOs, and the media reported incidents of excessive police searches in poor neighborhoods. During these operations police stopped and questioned persons and searched cars, residences, and business establishments without warrants.

Section 2. Respect for Civil Liberties, Including

a. Freedom of Speech and Press

The law and constitution provide for freedom of speech and press, and the authorities generally respected these rights. The independent media were active and expressed a wide variety of views with minimal restriction, but nongovernmental criminal elements continued to subject journalists to violence because of their professional activities. Despite national laws, politically motivated judicial censorship remained a problem within local-level courts. Some NGOs stated that press freedom declined during the year, citing increased instances of violence against journalists, mainly in the context of the massive demonstrations that shook the country in June and July and drew equally large- scale responses from security forces.

Violence and Harassment: The Brazilian Association of Radio and Television Broadcasters (ABERT) continued to report cases of imprisonment, aggression, censorship, and failure to respect freedom of the press. Between October 2012 and September 30, ABERT reported 136 cases of censorship, threats, direct violence against journalists, and other forms of pressure against news organizations and professionals. ABERT linked 105 of these cases to the numerous protests that occurred since June.

The SDH oversees the Program to Protect Human Rights Defenders, where threatened human rights activists, including journalists, can be placed under government protection. Eight states had their own programs (Bahia, Minas Gerais, Espirito Santo, Pernambuco, Rio de Janeiro, Para, Rio Grande do Sul, and Ceara). The federal government administered the program for states that lacked a program.

Within six weeks, gunmen allegedly killed two journalists in Ipatinga, a town of 250,000 inhabitants in Minas Gerais state. On March 8, assailants shot and killed Rodrigo Neto, a journalist who worked for a local newspaper, while he was in his car. On April 18, gunmen also shot and killed photojournalist

Walgney Assis Carvalho while he was fishing. At the end of November, authorities held 16 individuals, including civil policemen, in connection with the killings. Both Neto and Carvalho had reported on organized crime, specifically the formation of murder-for-hire death squads composed in part of off-duty policemen. In a March 19 visit to Minas Gerais state, Minister of Human Rights Maria do Rosario encouraged a full investigation of Neto's killing. Within one week of Carvalho's death, the state government replaced the Ipatinga chief of police as well as the civil police regional delegate. The Minas Gerais chief of Civil Police stated Carvalho had refused protection.

Censorship or Content Restrictions: The National Association of Newspapers, Brazilian Association for Journalism, and Inter American Press Association regarded the most serious threat to press freedom to be the growing number of cases of judicial censorship of the media. The NGOs noted the continuing trends of the media's dependence "on the political authorities at the state level" and court censorship orders.

Beginning in 2009, Fernando Sarney, son of federal senator Jose Sarney, repeatedly took the *Estado de S. Paulo* newspaper to court to prohibit the publication of reports linking him to official corruption, money laundering, and organized crime. In May the Fifth Civil State Court upheld censorship of the newspaper.

Nongovernmental Impact: During the year unidentified assailants killed at least six journalists, some apparently for their reporting. On June 11, unidentified gunmen shot and killed Jose Roberto Ornelas de Lemos, the director of the *Hora H* newspaper, who had reported on crime and corruption.

Internet Freedom

There were no government restrictions on access to the internet or credible reports that the government monitored e-mail or internet chat rooms without appropriate legal authority. Nevertheless, several legal and judicial rulings had the potential to threaten freedom of expression on the internet. A continuing trend was for private individuals and official bodies to take legal action against internet service providers and providers of online social media platforms, such as Google, Facebook, and Orkut, holding them accountable for content posted to or provided by users of the platform. Judicial rulings often resulted in the forced removal of content from the internet, and Google reported a 265 percent increase in content removal requests during the last half of 2012.

The electoral law regulates political campaigns on the internet. The rules prohibit candidates from buying advertising space online and restrict online campaign presences to websites operated by the candidate.

The International Telecommunication Union and the Center for Information and Communication Technologies Studies reported that 50 percent of the population used the internet and 40 percent of households had access to the internet in 2012. Only 10 percent of homes in rural areas had access to the internet, while 44 percent of homes in urban areas had access.

Academic Freedom and Cultural Events

There were no government restrictions on academic freedom or cultural events.

b. Freedom of Peaceful Assembly and Association

The law provides for freedom of assembly and association, and the government generally respected these rights.

Freedom of Assembly

During countrywide protests in June, security forces used rubber bullets, pepper spray, and tear gas against violent protesters, but in general security forces respected the right of peaceful protesters to freedom of assembly. Security forces occasionally used excessive force on peaceful protesters, particularly during protests in early June in Sao Paulo. In mid-June the federal government met with some protest group organizers to anticipate security needs for future protests, protect peaceful demonstrators, and limit violence.

c. Freedom of Religion

See the Department of State's *International Religious Freedom Report* at www.state.gov/j/drl/irf/rpt/.

d. Freedom of Movement, Internally Displaced Persons, Protection of Refugees, and Stateless Persons

The constitution provides for freedom of internal movement, foreign travel, emigration, and repatriation, and the government generally respected these rights. The government cooperated with the Office of the UN High Commissioner for Refugees (UNHCR) and other humanitarian organizations in providing protection and assistance to refugees, asylum seekers, and other persons of concern. In Sao Paulo an estimated 20 Sao Paulo businessmen from the Syrian-Brazilian community provided 19 immigrants fleeing unrest in Syria with housing, financial support, and translation services; traditional immigrant support groups, such as the federal government's National

Committee for Refugees, also provided assistance. The government provided documentation to new arrivals.

Protection of Refugees

Access to Asylum: The law provides for the granting of asylum or refugee status, and the government has established a system for providing protection to refugees. At year's end an estimated 4,690 refugees from approximately 79 countries were living in the country. From January to July, 1,600 immigrants requested refugee status. The UNHCR's country representative projected a total of 2,500 new refugees during the year, an increase from the 2,008 refugees granted asylum in 2012.

Temporary Protection: The government provided assistance to Haitian migrants who entered the country in hope of securing employment and relief from economic conditions in Haiti. The Haitians traveled through other countries in the region and requested asylum upon entering Brazil. The government did not find that the immigrants warranted refugee status but provided most of the more than 4,000 Haitians with humanitarian visas. The visas entitle them to receive health and social assistance, the right to work, and the right to remain for up to five years. The government also issued a special work visa through its consulate in Haiti for up to 1,200 persons a year to reduce the number of Haitians seeking entry through more dangerous migration routes. In August at least 40 pilgrims who came to Rio de Janeiro for the World (Catholic) Youth Day requested asylum. The pilgrims claimed they were fleeing violence and religious persecution in their homelands of Pakistan, Sierra Leone, and the Democratic Republic of the Congo.

Section 3. Respect for Political Rights: The Right of Citizens to Change Their Government

The law provides citizens the right to change their government peacefully, and citizens exercised this right through periodic, free, and fair elections based on universal suffrage. Military conscripts may not vote.

Elections and Political Participation

Recent Elections: In the 2010 national elections, which were considered free and fair, Workers' Party (PT) candidate Dilma Rousseff won a four-year term as president.

Participation of Women and Minorities: The law requires that at least 30 percent of the candidates registered by each political party be women, and most parties complied with the requirement. According to the Supreme Electoral Court, there were 3,968 female candidates in the 2010 elections, compared with 15,504 male candidates. Thirteen women were elected to the 81-member Senate and 44 women to the 513-member Chamber of Deputies. Of the 27 governors elected, two were women. Two of the 11 Federal Supreme Court justices were women.

In local elections held in 2012, a total of 7,648 women were elected to municipal councils (gaining 13 percent of the seats), and 663 female mayors were elected (12 percent of all mayors). There were 419,633 female council candidates, representing 32 percent of all candidates.

There were 44 Afro-Brazilians in Congress (one senator and 43 deputies) and one Afro-Brazilian each in the cabinet, Federal Supreme Court, and Superior Court of Justice. Joaquim Barbosa, the only Afro-Brazilian Supreme Court justice, began a two-year term as chief justice in 2012. Indigenous people's participation in politics was mostly limited to the local level.

Section 4. Corruption and Lack of Transparency in Government

The law provides criminal penalties for official corruption, but the government did not always implement the law effectively, and officials frequently engaged in corrupt practices with impunity. There were numerous reports of government corruption. During protests in June, corruption was one of the most widely cited concerns expressed, especially in regards to public spending on venues for the 2014 FIFA soccer World Cup and the 2016 Olympics.

Corruption: In November the Supreme Court remanded 17 of 25 individuals convicted in the Mensalao anticorruption trial to prison. Those incarcerated included former senior officials in the administration of former president Lula da Silva, including his chief of staff and PT president.

The Supreme Court also convicted two sitting members of Congress for corruption-related crimes. In June the court sentenced Congressman Natan Donadon to 13 years in prison on corruption-related crimes. In August the court remanded Senator Ivo Cassol to four years in semi-open confinement for procurement fraud.

On July 4, Congress passed law 039/2013, which creates civil and administrative penalties for Brazilian entities and legal persons that attempt to bribe foreign officials or engage in corrupt practices in Brazil or abroad. Individuals found to have engaged in such acts cannot win government contacts.

According to press reports, approximately 200 of the 594 members of Congress have had criminal cases before the Supreme Court, many for alleged acts of corruption.

Federal government entities such as the Federal Court of Audits, Federal Comptroller General, Public Ministry, Federal Police, judiciary, Department of Revenue and Control of Financial Activities, and Federal Treasury are responsible for fighting corruption. The agencies identified public spending as a source of financial corruption.

Whistleblower Protection: The law protects public servants but does not apply to employees at private companies. Public sector employers are prohibited from disciplining or terminating whistleblowers' employment.

Financial Disclosure: Public officials are subject to financial disclosure laws, and officials generally complied with these provisions. The Office of the Comptroller General serves as the executive branch agency mandated to monitor and verify disclosures. The Federal Court of Audits and the National Judicial Council, respectively, verify financial disclosure statements of employees in the judiciary and legislature. The Federal Revenue Office also can provide a public employee's asset declaration if that person is under investigation for illicit enrichment. While asset declarations are not made public, federal employees' salaries and payment information are posted online and can be searched by name. Such information became available on the government's transparency website when the new Law on Access to Public Information went into effect in June.

Public Access to Information: The law provides for public access to unclassified government information. The list of exceptions is sufficiently narrow and includes personal information; information that affects public safety or health, national security, or international relations; and sensitive military and intelligence information. The only fees charged are the costs of printing, copying, and mailing documentation. The government office has 20 days to respond to requests and can request an additional 10 days, for a maximum total of 30 days, after receiving the request. Agencies responded with full information 78 percent of the time within 11 days. Employees are subject to administrative sanctions for noncompliance and criminal charges if found to have fraudulently or deliberately destroyed or withheld information.

Section 5. Governmental Attitude Regarding International and Nongovernmental Investigation of Alleged Violations of Human Rights

A number of domestic and international human rights groups generally operated without government restriction, investigating and publishing their findings on human rights cases. Federal officials were cooperative and responsive to their views. Federal and state officials in many cases sought the aid and cooperation of domestic and international NGOs in addressing human rights problems; for instance, the Ministry of Labor (MTE) partnered with the International Labor Organization (ILO) to formulate national strategies for combating forced and child labor.

Government Human Rights Bodies: The Secretariat for Human Rights is an office under the presidency that holds ministerial-level rank. The secretariat has jurisdiction over issues regarding persons with disabilities, LGBT persons, the elderly, children, and government representation in international and regional human rights fora in conjunction with the Ministry of External Relations. The Chamber of Deputies and the Senate had human rights committees that operated without interference and participated in several activities nationwide in coordination with domestic and international human rights organizations. Marco Feliciano's appointment in March as president of the Chamber of Deputies' commission on human rights sparked controversy because of racist and homophobic comments he had made in the past, as well as his support for a law that would allow mental-health professionals to treat homosexuality as a mental disorder. Most states had police ombudsmen, but their accomplishments varied considerably, depending on such factors as funding and outside political pressure.

The National Truth Commission, established in 2011, continued its investigations into alleged human rights abuses committed from 1946 to 1988. Commission members met regularly to discuss progress on their specific areas of research. At a May seminar commemorating its first year of work, the commission released a formal progress report and demonstrated a prototype of the online application containing primary documents used by the commission to accompany the release of the final written report, due May 2014. Due to the volume of documents and witness testimony that still required analysis, the commission requested an extension of at least six months.

In July Pernambuco state's Truth Commission, in its first year of existence, reported the investigation of 51 cases of deaths and disappearances dating back to the military government. In two of these cases – including the case of Father Antonio Henrique, whose body was found with signs of torture in 1969 – the commission reached a provisional finding that the deaths were politically motivated.

Section 6. Discrimination, Societal Abuses, and Trafficking in Persons

The law prohibits and penalizes discrimination on the basis of race, gender, disability, or social status, but discrimination continued against women, Afro- Brazilians, indigenous persons, and LGBT persons.

Women

Rape and Domestic Violence: The law criminalizes rape, including spousal rape; sentences for convictions range from six to 30 years in prison. Domestic violence remained both widespread and underreported to the authorities, due to fear of retribution, further violence, and social stigma. The law stipulates a penalty of three months to three years in prison for persons who commit domestic violence, and authorities generally enforced the law effectively. Official statistics regarding the number of prosecutions and convictions were not available.

The federal government continued to operate a toll-free nationwide hotline for women. In 2012 the hotline registered 732,468 calls reporting domestic violence, 11 percent more than in 2011. Calls to the hotline leveled off after an initial surge, which government officials attributed to greater awareness among women of the hotline program. According to hotline data, 57 percent of the complaints received in 2012 concerned physical abuse. An international hotline service enabled Brazilian victims of gender-based violence to call in from Italy, Spain, and Portugal. In the first six months of the year, the international service received 90 calls, resulting in 33 women receiving assistance abroad.

In March President Rousseff launched the 265 million reais ($114.2 million) "Women, Living Without Violence" initiative to improve service to victims of gender-based violence. The program aims to increase the capacity of the women's hotline, provide more public health-care options for women, and construct 27 women's centers throughout the country that integrate specialized police, judicial, prosecutorial, health, employment, and other ministerial resources.

In January the Pernambuco State Technical Chamber for Combating Violence against Women began operations as part of a statewide public security initiative. The chamber is responsible for monitoring and reporting monthly to the governor all actions taken to promote the eradication of violence against women.

In April the Espirito Santo State Court of Justice and the city of Vitoria distributed a "panic button" device to 100 victims of domestic violence as part of the municipality's protection program. The device can send an alert with the victim's exact location to a monitoring center and also capture and record conversations that can be used as evidence in court.

A report by the Rio de Janeiro Public Security Institute revealed an increase in the number of reported rapes in the state. According to the report, from January to July there were 3,453 cases, compared with 2,928 during the same period in 2012. Authorities attributed the increase partly to victims' increased willingness to report assaults.

The Sao Paulo State Court of Justice created three new special courts of domestic and family violence against women. As of September the state of Sao Paulo had a total of 10 special courts to deal with domestic violence. As of July the courts had considered 35,959 cases, mostly related to threats of violence, rape, and coercion. There was no information available on the number of prosecutions or convictions.

Each state secretariat for public security operated police stations dedicated exclusively to addressing crimes against women. The 381 stations provided psychological counseling, temporary shelter, and hospital treatment for victims of domestic violence and rape, as well as criminal prosecution assistance by investigating incidents and forwarding evidence to courts. There were also 218 reference centers and 77 temporary women's shelters operated by state and local governments. The Secretariat for Women's Policies reported that fewer than 10 percent of municipalities had a dedicated space for the protection and care of victims of gender-based violence.

The Secretariat for Women's Policies published the Third National Plan on Women's Policies in August. The plan's main focus was to address gender inequality through public policies that promote the economic, cultural, and political autonomy of women in order to eradicate extreme poverty and enable full participation in society. The Secretariat for Women's Policies acted as the coordinating agency for all actions carried out under the Third National Plan and evaluated the end results across government organs.

The law requires health facilities to contact the police about cases in which a woman was harmed physically, sexually, or psychologically to collect evidence and statements should the victim decide to prosecute.

The Chamber of Deputies' Special Office of Women's Promotion remained active. The office undertakes surveys and studies on the situation of women, specifically pertaining to gender-based violence; works with international organizations and NGOs to share best practices; and heads a network of protection for victims of gender-based violence in conjunction with NGOs, state, and local governments. In March the Senate approved the creation of its own Special Office of Women's Promotion.

A study on gender-based violence (GBV) published by the Institute for Applied Economic Research reported that between 2009 and 2011, the country registered nearly six killings for every 100,000 women. The states of Espirito Santo, Bahia, and Alagoas had the highest levels of GBV-related killings, with 11 deaths per 100,000 women. The study also compared data on GBV-related homicides before and after the 2006 passage of the Maria da Penha law to reduce domestic violence and found that GBV rates had remained stable since 2001.

Sexual Harassment: Sexual harassment is a criminal offense, punishable by up to two years in prison. The law encompasses sexual advances in the workplace or educational institutions and between service providers or clients. In the workplace it applies only in hierarchical situations where the harasser is of higher rank or position than the victim. The government generally enforced sexual harassment laws effectively. No official data were available on the prevalence of sexual harassment in the workplace, but in a survey conducted by the Sao Paulo Secretary's Union, 25 percent of secretaries in the state claimed to have been sexually harassed by their supervisors.

Reproductive Rights: Couples and individuals have the right to decide the number, spacing, and timing of children and had the information and means to do so free from discrimination, coercion, and violence. Access to information on contraception; skilled attendance at delivery; and prenatal, postpartum, and essential obstetric care generally were available. According to the 2013 UN Population Fund report, skilled health personnel assisted in 99 percent of births.

Discrimination: The cabinet-level Secretariat for Women's Policies supervises a special entity charged with overseeing the legal rights of women. Women's labor force participation (75 percent) was below that of men (85 percent), and women were more likely to work in the informal sector. Although the law prohibits discrimination based on gender in employment and wages, the IBGE reported that in 2011 women received 72 percent of the income of men for comparable work.

Children

Birth Registration: Citizenship is derived from birth in the country or from a parent. According to 2010 IBGE census data, there were approximately 599,000 unregistered children nationwide. Without birth certificates children cannot be vaccinated or enrolled in school. If the problem persisted into adulthood, an unregistered adult could not obtain a worker's card or receive retirement benefits.

The CNJ, in partnership with the SDH, aimed to reduce the number of such children by registering children born in maternity wards. The National Documentation of Rural Workers initiative offered assistance in obtaining identification cards, birth certificates for children born in rural areas, labor cards, and tax documents. From 2004 to the end of 2012, more than 920,600 women and children had been documented through the program.

Child Abuse: Abuse and neglect of children and adolescents were problems and included rape, molestation, and impregnation of girls by family members. The SDH oversaw the National Program to Confront Sexual Violence against Children and Adolescents, which established nationwide strategies for combating child sexual abuse and best practices for treating victims.

From January to November, the SDH-operated Dial 100, a hotline for complaints of sexual abuse against children and adolescents, logged 35,140 complaints, compared with 19,946 during all of 2011. According to the SDH, the rise was due to increased national awareness of what constituted sexual abuse and sexual exploitation.

The NGO Social Service for Industry operated child protective centers in 21 cities in 17 states. The program served 3.5 million adolescents between the ages of 16 and 21, who received psychological counseling, medical attention, legal advice, and technical schooling.

According to data released by the National Register of Sheltered Children and the Public Ministry, there were approximately 45,600 children and adolescents living in 4,029 shelters provided by NGOs, churches, and other religious organizations throughout the country. The Public Ministry released data in August claiming that one-third of the sheltered children exceeded the two years they were allowed by law to reside in shelters and that 86 percent of children in shelters had families they could rejoin after two years.

The Death Threat Protection Program for Children and Adolescents brought in 1,501 children and adolescents and 2,230 families in 2011, the latest period for which data were available. A majority of those shielded by the program had received death threats due to involvement in drug trafficking, and most entered the program accompanied by one or more family members. The program offered psychological counseling and technical courses to reinsert these youth into stable community situations. The Index of Youth Homicides produced by the SDH and the UN Children's Fund (UNICEF) reported that homicides accounted for 45 percent of the deaths of adolescents between 12 and 18 years of age.

Forced and Early Marriage: The legal minimum age of marriage is 18 (age 16 with parental or legal representative consent). According to UNICEF, approximately 36 percent of women 20-24 years of age were married or in a union before age 18.

Sexual Exploitation of Children: The law sets a minimum age of 14 for consensual sex, with the penalty for statutory rape ranging from eight to15 years in prison. The country was a destination for child sex tourism. Several major coastal cities in the northeast served as tourist destinations for the sexual exploitation of children and adolescents. While no specific laws address child sex tourism, it is punishable under other criminal offenses. According to data from the SDH, University of Brasilia, UNICEF, and ILO, more than 100,000 children were victims of sexual exploitation each year.

The SDH continued its national internet campaign against sexual abuse and sexual exploitation of children and adolescents. With a focus on prevention, the goal of the program was to raise awareness prior to the annual carnival season and the FIFA soccer World Cup.

The law criminalizes child pornography. The penalty for possession of child pornography is up to four years in prison and a fine. Those who produce, reproduce, or offer for sale child pornography or recruit a child to participate in a pornographic production may be imprisoned up to eight years and fined.

Although the country is not a large-scale producer of child pornography, such material was spread on social networking websites. The Public Ministry, Dial 100, and the NGO Safernet, in partnership with the Federal Police, registered 10,715 child pornography complaints between January 1 and July 1, compared with 19,311 complaints in the same period in 2011. From January to August, authorities imprisoned 41 individuals for disseminating child pornography on the internet.

The Ministry of Tourism continued to promote its code of conduct to prevent the commercial sexual exploitation of children in the tourism industry. The Federal Highway Police and the ILO continued to disseminate awareness materials in places such as gas stations, bars, restaurants, motels, and nightclubs along highways considered areas for sexual exploitation of children and adolescents. Despite these efforts, a Federal Highway Police study found 1,776 hotspots for child prostitution throughout the country, mainly at major highway intersections close to urban areas. The study also found that since 2006, the authorities had removed 3,812 children and adolescents from these hotspots and taken 1,662 individuals into custody for crimes against minors.

International Child Abductions: The country is a party to the 1980 Hague Convention on the Civil Aspects of International Child Abduction. For information see the Department of State's report on compliance at www.travel.state.gov/abduction/resources/congressreport/congressreport_4308.html as well as country-specific information at http://www.travel.state.gov/abduction/country/country_5886.html.

Anti-Semitism

According to the Jewish Federation, there were approximately 125,000 Jewish citizens, of whom approximately 65,000 were in the state of Sao Paulo and 40,000 in Rio de Janeiro state. It is illegal to write, edit, publish, or sell books that promote anti-Semitism or racism. The law enables courts to fine or imprison anyone who displays, distributes, or broadcasts anti-Semitic materials and mandates a two- to five-year prison term.

In the city of Sao Paulo, there were isolated incidents of anti-Semitism, including physical and verbal attacks against Jewish persons, anti-Semitic graffiti, and displays of neo-Nazism.

According to a study conducted by the State University of Campinas (Sao Paulo), neo-Nazi groups that traditionally operated in the southern states of Rio Grande do Sul, Santa Catarina, and Parana began to grow in the past decade in Federal District and Minas Gerais State. The study estimated that there were approximately 105,000 neo-Nazis in the three southern states and 29,000 in Sao Paulo state.

Trafficking in Persons

See the Department of State's *Trafficking in Persons Report* at www.state.gov/j/tip/.

Persons with Disabilities

The law prohibits discrimination against persons with physical and mental disabilities in employment, air travel and other transportation, education, and access to health care, and the federal government effectively enforced these provisions. An estimated 10 percent of the population had some form of disability. While federal and state laws mandate access to buildings for persons with disabilities, states did not enforce them effectively. A 1991 federal law requires private companies to hire disabled individuals at a minimum level of 2 percent of their workforce, but authorities did not effectively enforce this quota.

The National Council for the Rights of Persons with Disabilities and the National Council for the Rights of the Elderly, both within the SDH, have primary responsibility for promoting the rights of persons with disabilities. According to the SDH, specific problems included the short supply of affordable and up-to-date orthotics and prosthetics, scarcity of affordable housing with special adaptations, and a need for greater accessibility to public transport. Children with disabilities attended school (primary, secondary, and higher education), but there existed a shortage of schools with facilities for such persons. The absence of accessible infrastructure and schools had a significant impact within the workforce, and only an estimated 6 percent of the population with disabilities participated in the workforce.

The city government of Teresina, the state capital of Piaui, also funded infrastructure investments to improve mobility and access for the disabled community; it allocated roughly 1.7 million reais ($733,000) in public funds to improve city streets and sidewalks to make them more accessible for disabled persons.

The government improved access for persons with disabilities in its infrastructure development and in retrofitting public sports venues to prepare for the upcoming sporting events, including the 2016 Paralympics games.

National/Racial/Ethnic Minorities

The law prohibits racial discrimination, specifically the denial of public or private facilities, employment, or housing, to anyone based on race. The law also prohibits, and stipulates prison terms for, the incitement of racial discrimination or prejudice and the dissemination of racially offensive symbols and epithets. The 2010 census reported that for the first time white persons constituted less than half the population of 190.8 million, since a total of 99.7 million persons identified themselves as belonging to categories other than white. Despite laws and a high representation within the general population, darker-skinned citizens, particularly Afro-Brazilians, frequently encountered discrimination.

In August Teodoro Lalor de Lima, leader of a community of descendants of escaped slaves (quilombo), was stabbed to death in Belem, Para state. Lalor de Lima fought for the rights of quilombos and had received threats for his advocacy of quilombo communities' land rights. The Civil Police continued to investigate the killing.

Afro-Brazilians continued to be underrepresented in the government, professional positions, and middle and upper classes. They experienced a higher rate of unemployment and earned average wages below those of whites in similar positions. There was also a sizeable education gap. Afro-Brazilians were disproportionately negatively affected by crime, and black males were twice as likely as their white counterparts to be homicide victims.

The 2010 Racial Equality Statute continued to be controversial, due to its provision for nonquota affirmative action policies in education and employment. In 2012 the Supreme Court upheld racial quota systems at universities as constitutional, and a quotas law went into effect that gave the 59 federal universities four years to ensure that half of their incoming classes be from public schools, which generally served poorer students. Departments within the Federal University of Rio de Janeiro and the University of Brasilia also began to implement quotas for racial minorities in their master's and doctoral programs. Between 2001 and 2011, college attendance rates increased from 10 percent to 36 percent for black and mixed-race students ages 18 to 24.

In addition to the quota system, in May the Ministry of Education announced a stipend for students in federal universities who met certain income and racial requirements. Students from low income families earning less than 1,017 reais per month ($438) would be eligible to receive 400 reais ($172) per month, while students from indigenous and quilombo communities (communities of descendants of escaped slaves) could receive 900 reais ($388) per month.

Indigenous People

According to data from the National Indigenous Foundation (FUNAI), National Health Foundation, and the 2010 census, there were approximately 897,000 indigenous persons (0.5 percent of the national population), representing 305 distinct indigenous ethnic groups and 274 languages. Approximately 17,000 lived in 4,672 formally recognized indigenous zones, covering 12.5 percent of the national territory. Approximately 8 percent of the indigenous lands are concentrated in the Amazon region.

The law grants the indigenous population broad protection of their cultural patrimony, exclusive use of their traditional lands, and exclusive beneficial use of their territory. After consulting with the tribes involved, Congress must approve each request to exploit water resources, including ones with energy potential and minerals on indigenous lands. The law grants indigenous tribes rights to a portion of the profit resulting from mining. According to the constitution, all aboveground and underground minerals as well as hydroelectric-power potential belong to the government. The construction of the Belo Monte dam, one of the largest hydroelectric projects undertaken by the government, led to frequent conflicts with nearby indigenous communities. At times this resulted in conflict with security forces, which occasionally led to violence. The ILO and IACHR ruled that the project violated the government's international agreements on indigenous rights, and the UN Special Rapporteur on the Rights of Indigenous Peoples expressed similar concerns in his reporting.

The Maraiwatsede reserve, home to the Xavante indigenous group in the state of Mato Grosso, was demarcated in 1998, yet nonindigenous settlers continued to reside illegally in the reserve. While the 1988 constitution charged the federal government with demarcating indigenous areas within five years, the government had not completed the four phases of demarcation (identification, declaration, approval, and registration) by yearend. In August fires destroyed one-fifth of the Maraiwatsede reserve; some officials attributed the fires to soybean farmers and cattle ranchers taking revenge for their 2012 eviction from the lands.

In April a special commission began to analyze a constitutional amendment that would transfer the ability to demarcate indigenous territories from FUNAI to Congress, causing indigenous protesters to enter congressional hearings without permission at various times in the ensuing months. In May President Rousseff's chief of staff, Gleisi Hoffmann, stated that FUNAI did not have the capacity to mediate conflicts between indigenous people and rural landowners and that the government would explore including other government agencies in the decision- making process for demarcating indigenous lands. Since 2010 the government has cut funding to FUNAI by 67.8 percent to 5.9 million reais ($2.5million).

According to a June report released by the Indigenous Missionary Council, 60 indigenous persons were killed in 2012, 11 more than in 2011. In addition 1,054 indigenous persons suffered death threats and attempts on their lives. Mato Grosso do Sul state registered more than one-half of all indigenous homicides, with 37 deaths. Most of the violence against indigenous people was connected to contentious land demarcation disputes. For example, gunmen killed two indigenous persons in Mato Grosso do Sul in June. The Indigenous Missionary Council attributed the killings to the Guarani-Kaiowa peoples' desire to expand their territory, located on the border with Paraguay and next to three cattle ranches. According to the National Committee to Combat Rural Violence, an organization linked to the federal government, illegal evictions from demarcated lands by armed ranchers and farmers, often bearing forged documents, were among the main causes of violence against indigenous people.

Societal Abuses, Discrimination, and Acts of Violence Based on Sexual Orientation and Gender Identity

Federal law does not prohibit discrimination based on sexual orientation, but several states and municipalities have administrative regulations that prohibit such discrimination and provide for equal access to government services.

In June the SDH released its *Second Annual Report on Homophobic Violence*, which stated that in 2012 there were 315 LGBT-related homicides, compared with 278 in 2011. The NGO Rainbow Group considered the SDH report more accurate than the information in other annual reports on homophobic violence because of its use of government data as well as media reports.

According to the SDH, many transgender individuals had difficulty entering the formal labor market or study programs because an apparent discrepancy between the photograph on an individual's labor card and an individual's personal appearance prevented some from obtaining permission to work.

The National LGBT Council, created in 2010 to combat discrimination and promote the rights of LGBT people, continued to meet every two months. Meetings were open to the public and broadcast over the internet. During the year the SDH launched the National System to Promote LGBT Rights and Confront Violence against LGBT Persons, with the purpose of promoting public policies to mitigate discrimination affecting the LGBT community. In August the states of Goias, Minas Gerais, and Rio Grande do Sul began registering cases of homophobic violence.

A 1999 resolution of the Federal Council of Psychology prohibited psychological professionals from offering services that treated homosexuality as a mental illness. Federal Deputy Marco Feliciano, president of the Chamber of Deputies' Human Rights and Minorities Commission, sparked controversy by supporting legislation that would lift these restrictions and allow psychological professionals to offer treatment to homosexual patients seeking to reorient their sexuality. The Chamber of Deputies blocked the proposed law.

On June 4, Rio de Janeiro's state-run program "Rio without Homophobia" began a second round of diversity training for police officers, focusing on the rights of LGBT persons. Five thousand officers stationed in the city of Rio participated in the first training session.

The state of Pernambuco sponsored a "human rights road show" program, the first of its kind in the country. The road show visits often led to increased reporting of crimes against the LGBT community. On June 25, the governor of Pernambuco signed a decree creating a data center to register statistics on cases of homophobic violence in the state. The center was required to record and report every 12 months all information on cases of violence against the LGBT community.

Other Societal Violence or Discrimination

Sao Paulo Governor Geraldo Alckmin announced an involuntary drug treatment program on January 11, in response to the rising use of crack cocaine and the spread of drug markets known as "cracolandias," where addicts consumed the drug openly on the streets. The new program allowed state health workers or family members of addicts in "advanced stages" of addiction and at risk of death to recommend court-ordered treatment without the consent of the patient. A judge and a state-appointed doctor would then decide whether to commit patients to treatment centers. According to a Federal University of Sao Paulo study, there were more than one million crack cocaine users in the country.

Violence connected to environmental activism and agrarian conflicts continued. According to the Catholic NGO Pastoral Land Commission, 36 individuals lost their lives in killings linked to land- and water-rights conflicts that occurred in remote areas in 2012, a 24 percent increase from 2011. Seventeen of the killings occurred in the north, including nine in the state of Rondonia.

In August a judge in Minas Gerais state ordered four men implicated in the killings of five land reform activists to be placed in preventive custody. The judge handed down the order due to threats against potential jury members and witnesses as well as repeated efforts by the defense lawyer to delay the trial. The case continued at year's end.

On May 14, the Supreme Court overturned the conviction of Vitalmiro Bastos de Moura, accused of ordering the 2005 murder of Catholic nun Dorothy Mae Stang, and ordered a fourth trial after determining Moura's lawyer lacked sufficient time to prepare his defense. On September 19, the court again convicted Moura of ordering the murder of Dorothy Stang and sentenced him to 30 years in prison. In July, Rayfran das Neves Sales, the gunman who killed Dorothy Stang, was released from prison on parole after serving eight years of his 27-year sentence.

There were no reported cases of societal violence or discrimination against persons with HIV/AIDS.

Section 7. Worker Rights

a. Freedom of Association and the Right to Collective Bargaining

The law provides for freedom of association for all workers (except members of the military, uniformed police, and firefighters) but limits organizing at the enterprise level and imposes a mandatory union tax on workers and employers. The law provides for the right to strike except for the armed forces, military police, and firefighters. Civil police are allowed to conduct strikes. The law prohibits antiunion discrimination, including the dismissal of employees who are candidates for, or holders of, union leadership positions, and it requires employers to reinstate workers fired for union activity.

New unions must register with the MTE, which accepts the registration unless objections are filed by other unions. The law stipulates certain restrictions, such as "unicidade" (in essence one union per city), which limits freedom of association by prohibiting multiple, competing unions of the same professional category in a given geographical area. Unions that represent workers in the same geographical area and professional category may contest registration. If the objection is found to be valid, the MTE does not register the union. While a number of competing unions existed, the MTE and courts enforced unicidade in decisions regarding the registration of new unions. Most elements of the labor movement and the International Trade Union Confederation criticized unicidade.

The law stipulates that a strike may be ruled "abusive" by labor courts and be punishable if a number of conditions are not met, such as maintaining essential services during a strike, notifying employers at least 48 hours before the beginning of a walkout, and ending a strike after a labor court decision.

Employers may not hire substitute workers during a legal strike or fire workers for strike-related activity, provided the strike is not ruled abusive.

The law obliges a union to negotiate on behalf of all registered workers in the professional category and geographical area it represents, regardless of whether an employee pays voluntary membership dues. The law permits the government to reject clauses of collective bargaining agreements that conflict with government policy. Collective bargaining is effectively prohibited in the public sector; the constitution allows it, but implementing legislation had not been enacted.

Authorities at times did not effectively enforce laws protecting freedom of association and collective bargaining. Penalties under the law ranging from 10 reais to 1,000 reais ($4.31 to $431) were generally sufficient to deter violations, and labor courts enforced payments. Parties generally agreed that the courts decided cases fairly.

Freedom of association was generally respected. Collective bargaining was widespread in formal sector establishments of the private sector. Worker organizations were independent of the government and political parties, and there was no government interference in union activities. Intimidation and killings of rural union organizers and their agents continued. For example, on March 21, an unidentified assailant shot and killed Fatima Benites, president of the Union of Workers and Rural Workers of Bela Vista, Mato Grosso do Sul, close to the union headquarters.

Employers fired strike organizers for reasons ostensibly unrelated to strikes. Legal recourse related to retaliatory discharge, although improving, was often a protracted process.

b. Prohibition of Forced or Compulsory Labor

The labor law prohibits what it calls "slave labor," defined as "reducing someone to a condition analogous to slavery," including subjecting someone to forced labor as well to exploitative working conditions in general, such as long workdays, unhygienic work conditions, extremely arduous labor, and labor performed in degrading working conditions. The government took a number of actions to enforce the law, although forced labor continued to occur in a number of states. Violators of forced labor laws face sentences of up to eight years in prison. The law also provides penalties for various crimes related to forced labor, such as recruiting or transporting workers or obliging them to incur debt as part of a forced labor scheme.

The National Commission to Eradicate Slave Labor coordinated government efforts to combat forced and exploitative labor and provided a forum for input from civil society. During 2012, the latest year for which such data were available, the MTE reported removing 2,428 laborers from "conditions analogous to slavery" in 164 unannounced inspections of 331properties. The government uses the terms "slave labor" and "conditions analogous to slavery" under the broader definition of forced or poor labor conditions. It was unclear how many of these cases involved forced labor as opposed to degrading labor conditions.

The MTE's Mobile Inspection Unit teams conducted surprise inspections of properties on which forced labor was suspected or reported, using teams composed of labor inspectors, labor prosecutors from the Federal Labor Prosecutor's Office, and Federal Police officers. Mobile teams levied fines on landowners who used forced labor and required employers to provide back pay and benefits to workers before returning the workers to their municipalities of origin. Workers removed by mobile units were entitled to three months' salary at the minimum wage. The MTE ordered employers to pay 9.9 million reais ($4.27 million) in back pay in 2012. Few specialized services were provided to these workers, and NGOs noted a high revictimization rate.

The government continued to partner with the ILO in projects to eradicate forced labor and promote decent work in the states of Mato Grosso, Bahia, and Sao Paulo.

The MTE also published a "dirty list" to expose publicly employers (persons or legal entities) caught using forced labor. The list was updated every six months by the MTE's Secretariat of Labor Inspections and was available on the MTE website. Inclusion on the "dirty list" had serious financial consequences in that public financial institutions as well as many private banks deny credit and other services to listed individuals and companies. As of November the list contained 488 names.

During the year the Sao Paulo state government approved legislation to combat forced and exploitative labor in supply chains. The law provides for a 10-year revocation of the business license of any entity that directly or indirectly employs workers under forced labor conditions.

Efforts against forced labor were hindered by failure to impose effective penalties, the remoteness of the area where the crime typically occurred, lack of awareness of rights, delays in judicial procedure that resulted in de facto impunity for those responsible, and lack of sufficient programs to assist victims of forced labor. Accurate, nationwide statistics on prosecutions for forced labor cases were not available. In September a federal court in Sao Paulo sentenced Ronaldo Perao to seven years and six months in prison for subjecting 21 employees to "conditions analogous to slavery" on his coffee plantation in 2011. The defendant was not imprisoned and planned to appeal the conviction.

Efforts of the federal government were supported by a number of state initiatives, and several states have state commissions for the eradication of forced labor, including Tocantins, Bahia, Rio de Janeiro, Sao Paulo, Mato Grosso do Sul, Para, Maranhao, Mato Grosso, and Rio Grande do Sul. The Sao Paulo State Commission for the Eradication of Forced Labor (COETRAE) met regularly during the year under the coordination of the Secretariat of Justice. The commission, created in September 2011, functioned in tandem with the Sao Paulo Nucleus to Combat Trafficking in Persons. COETRAE was composed of members from the Secretariats of Justice, Labor, Agriculture, Environment, Treasury, and Education and also from the Public Ministry, police forces, and NGOs. The commission focused exclusively on cases of forced labor as well as what the law terms "conditions analogous to slavery."

On March 14, nine members of the Mato Grosso state COETRAE left the commission due to the perceived ineffectiveness of the organization. In a letter signed by various commission participants including unions, the Pastoral Land Commission, judges, and the Federal Public Ministry, among others, the former members complained of frequent cancellations of meetings, the lack of an updated State Pan to Eradicate Forced Labor, and comments made by Mato Grosso government officials questioning the validity of MTE's "dirty list."

Forced labor, including by children, occurred in many states, in work such as clearing forest to provide cattle pastureland, logging, charcoal production, raising livestock, and other agricultural activities. Forced labor often involved young men drawn from the less-developed northeastern states – Maranhao, Piaui, Tocantins, Para, and Ceara – and the central state of Goias to work in the northern and central- western regions of the country. In addition there were reports of forced labor in the construction industry also involving young men principally from the northeast. Cases of forced labor were also reported in sweatshops in the city of Sao Paulo; the victims were often from neighboring countries, particularly Bolivia and Paraguay. In August labor inspectors removed 13 Bolivian workers and four children from a sweatshop in Sao Paulo where they worked for upwards of 13 hours a day and were forced to live where they worked. In 2012 the Pernambuco Labor Prosecutor's Office found and removed 33 workers in forced labor conditions; 21 of them worked in sugar mills and six in the construction industry.

The coordinator of the National Campaign to Combat Slave Labor (linked to the Public Ministry of Labor) estimated that there were between 20,000 and 50,000 laborers working in "conditions analogous to slavery" at any given time during the year. According to the Pastoral Land Commission's 2012 report published in May, there were 168 incidents in which people were found in "conditions analogous to slavery." States with the highest number of removed workers were Mato Grosso, Goias, Amapa, Para, Maranhao, and Tocantins. The primary economic activities where forced labor was found included ranching, charcoal making, and farming. Forced labor in domestic servitude involving women and adolescents (the latter typically working with their parents) was also reported.

Also see the Department of State's *Trafficking in Persons Report* at www.state.gov/j/tip/.

c. Prohibition of Child Labor and Minimum Age for Employment

The minimum working age is 16 years, and apprenticeships may begin at age 14. The law bars all minors under age 18 from work that constitutes a physical strain or occurs in unhealthy, dangerous, or morally harmful conditions. Hazardous work includes an extensive list of activities within 13 occupational categories, including domestic service, garbage scavenging, and fertilizer production. The law requires parental permission for minors to work as apprentices.

The MTE is responsible for inspecting worksites to enforce child labor laws. Penalties for violations ranged from 402 reais to 2,013 reais ($173 to $868), doubling for a second violation and tripling for a third, and were sufficient to deter violations and were generally enforced; however, NGOs asserted that fines were usually too small to serve as an effective deterrent. Most inspections of children in the workplace were driven by complaints brought by workers, teachers, unions, NGOs, and the media. Labor inspectors remained unable to enter private homes and farms, where much of the nation's child labor occurred.

The government implemented innovative programs to prevent child labor, including the Program to Eradicate Child Labor (PETI), coordinated by the Ministry of Social Development and Combating Hunger with state and local authorities. Through PETI, families with children seven to 15 years of age working in selected hazardous activities received monthly cash stipends to keep their children in school. PETI serviced more than 820,000 children in 3,500 municipalities. Also through the ministry, the Bolsa Familia program provided a monthly stipend to low-income families that kept their children up to age 17 in school and met certain child health requirements. The Bolsa Familia served more than 13 million households nationwide. Beyond the Bolsa Familia, the government operated the Brasil Sem Miseria (Brazil without

Misery) and Brasil Carinhoso (Caring Brazil) programs to build on programs such as the Bolsa Familia as well as to provide access to public services and to stimulate employment opportunities. The government also continued to partner with the ILO in projects to eradicate child labor in the state of Mato Grosso. The Federal Police also expended funds to respond to criminal cases involving forced child labor.

Nevertheless, child labor continued to be a problem. The 2011 IBGE National Household Survey, reflecting the most recent data available, showed that 4.28 million of an estimated 44 million children between the ages of five and 17 were engaged in some form of child labor, more than 250,000 of whom were domestic workers. Of the minors engaged in child labor, children between the ages of five and nine made up 2 percent of the child labor population, children 10 to 14 made up 27.5 percent, and children 15 to 17 made up 70.5 percent. According to 2010 data from the MTE, the majority of the children were employed in street vending (42 percent), followed by automobile washing (10 percent), manufacturing (8 percent), and agriculture (3 percent).

According to a study conducted by the daily newspaper *Folha de Sao Paulo* and based on 2010 census data, the incidence of child labor was more prevalent in the north, where one in 10 children worked, either in paid or unpaid jobs. The 2010 census reported that 132,000 children between the ages 10 and 14 were the sole providers for their families. Approximately one-half of child laborers received no income, and 90 percent worked in the unregistered informal sector. Slightly more than one-half of child laborers worked in rural areas. The study also found that 95 percent of the children who worked also attended school.

According to MTE data, 5,000 children and adolescents were found in situations that violated minimum-age laws in 6,387 unannounced inspections from January to September. A majority, 81 percent, of those found were young boys. In 2012 a total of 7,393 inspections discovered 7,124 children and adolescents employed in violation of minimum-age laws.

Children worked in agriculture, including in raising livestock and in the production of cashews, coffee, sugarcane, cotton, manioc, pineapple, sisal, soybeans, rice, and tobacco. Children were also involved in the production of ceramics, bricks, charcoal, and footwear.

Also see the Department of Labor's *Findings on the Worst Forms of Child Labor* at www.dol.gov/ilab/programs/ocft/tda.htm.

d. Acceptable Conditions of Work

In January the minimum wage increased to 678 reais ($292) per month. According to 2010 IBGE data, the most recent information available, the per capita income of approximately 50 percent of the population was below the minimum wage. IGBE data also revealed that 8.5 percent of inhabitants (16.2 million) were considered "extremely poor" or earning less than 70 reais ($30) per month.

The law limits the work week to 44 hours and specifies a weekly rest period of 24 consecutive hours, preferably on Sundays. The law also provides for paid annual vacation, prohibits excessive compulsory overtime, limits overtime to two hours per workday, and stipulates that hours worked above the monthly limit must be compensated with at least time-and-a-half pay; these provisions generally were enforced for all groups of workers in the formal sector.

The MTE sets occupational, health, and safety standards that are consistent with internationally recognized norms, although unsafe working conditions were prevalent throughout the country, especially in construction. Accidents at large construction projects for the FIFA soccer World Cup, such as stadiums and infrastructure, prompted slightly improved enforcement of safety regulations. The law requires employers to establish internal committees for accident prevention in workplaces. It also provides for the protection of employees from being fired for their committee activities.

As part of its efforts to combat forced labor, the MTE's Mobile Inspection Unit teams also addressed issues related to acceptable conditions of work such as long workdays and unsafe or unhygienic work conditions. At the end of 2012, the MTE employed a total of 2,995 labor inspectors, slightly down from 3,085 at the end of 2011. Penalties for violations included fines and were generally enforced. In March the MTE announced the creation of the National Labor Inspection School for the training of labor inspectors throughout the country.

In August labor inspectors removed 40 workers from an orange plantation in the interior of Sao Paulo state. The landowner subjected the workers to long work days, insufficient salaries, and degrading living conditions. One pair of workers lived in a converted chicken coop. The landowner owed each worker 20,000 reais ($8,620) as well as the cost of transportation back to their cities of origin.

Irregularities in the work conditions of Bolivian immigrants working in the garment industry, principally in Sao Paulo, continued in 2012. In July, 28 labor inspectors removed Bolivian immigrant workers from degrading work conditions in a sweatshop in Sao Paulo run by textile manufacturing company Restoque, which produced clothes for the popular Le Lis Blanc and Bourgeois Boheme brands. The company signed an agreement with the Public Ministry of Labor to change its labor practices as well as pay one million reais ($431,000) for moral damages that could keep Restoque off the "dirty list." The company complied immediately with the agreement and said that the sweatshops in question were run by a third-party contractor.

According to IBGE data, there were approximately 44.2 million persons in the informal sector in 2011, the most recent year for which data were available. Most unregistered workers were in the agricultural sector. Not all foreign migrant workers, informal sector workers, and unregistered workers were subject to hazardous working conditions, but these groups were at a higher risk of being subjected to exploitative conditions.

In 2012 there were approximately 724,000 workplace accidents and 2,731 workplace fatalities. On October 1, the Labor Court halted construction at the Arena da Baixada stadium in Curitiba, one of the sites set to host World Cup games in 2014. Judge Lorraine Colnago found conditions at the stadium to be dangerous for workers and fined the Brazilian Football League reais ($215,500) per day for failure to comply with labor laws.

In: Brazil: Conditions, Issues and U.S. Relations ISBN: 978-1-63321-253-4
Editor: Julia Sutton

Chapter 3

BRAZIL 2012 INTERNATIONAL RELIGIOUS FREEDOM REPORT*

U.S. Department of State;
Bureau of Democracy, Human Rights and Labor

EXECUTIVE SUMMARY

The constitution and other laws and policies protect religious freedom and, in practice, the government respected religious freedom. The trend in the government's respect for religious freedom did not change significantly during the year.

There were some reports of societal discrimination based on religious affiliation, belief, or practice, including incidents involving anti-Semitism and intolerance toward members of Africa-based religious groups. Prominent societal leaders took positive steps to promote religious freedom and interfaith understanding among Christians, Muslims, Jews, and members of other religious groups.

The U.S. embassy and consulates actively engaged with civil society groups and nongovernmental organizations (NGOs) to facilitate interfaith dialogue and promote religious tolerance. Outreach efforts included meetings with religious leaders and participation in interfaith events.

---

* This document was released by the U.S. Department of State; Bureau of Democracy, Human Rights and Labor in 2013.

SECTION I. RELIGIOUS DEMOGRAPHY

According to the 2010 census, the population is 190.7 million. An estimated 64.6 percent of the population is Roman Catholic and 22 percent is Protestant. Approximately 60 percent of Protestants belong to Pentecostal churches, 18 percent belong to traditional Protestant churches, and 22 percent to other Protestant groups. Other Christian groups constituting less than 1 percent of the population include Jehovah's Witnesses and The Church of Jesus Christ of Latter-day Saints (Mormons).

Other groups constituting less than 1 percent each include African and syncretic religious groups such as Candomble and Umbanda, Buddhists, Jews, Muslims, and Hindus. There is a small number of adherents of indigenous religious beliefs.

There are different assessments of the number of Muslims. According to the 2010 census, there are approximately 35,200 Muslims, while the Federation of Muslim Associations of Brazil considers the number to be about 1.5 million. Other observers estimate there are approximately 400,000-500,000 Muslims. There are significant Muslim communities in the cities of Sao Paulo, Rio de Janeiro, Curitiba, and Foz do Iguazu, as well as in smaller cities in the states of Parana, Rio Grande do Sul, Sao Paulo, and Rio de Janeiro.

According to the Jewish Confederation of Brazil, there are more than 125,000 Jews, 65,000 of whom reside in Sao Paulo State and 40,000 in Rio de Janeiro State. Many other cities have smaller Jewish communities.

SECTION II. STATUS OF GOVERNMENT RESPECT FOR RELIGIOUS FREEDOM

Legal/Policy Framework

The constitution and other laws and policies protect religious freedom. The law provides penalties of up to five years in prison for crimes of religious intolerance. Courts may fine or imprison for two to five years anyone who displays, distributes, or broadcasts religiously intolerant material. It is illegal to write, edit, publish, or sell literature that promotes religious intolerance, including anti-Semitism.

The Racial Equality Act provides for the right to practice religions of African origin. By law, members of religions of African origin must have access to religious professionals in hospitals, prisons, and other institutions.

There are no registration requirements for religious groups. Religious groups are free to establish places of worship, train clergy, and proselytize. There is a general provision for access to religious services and counsel in all civil and military establishments. The law prohibits discrimination based on religion.

Public schools are required to offer religious instruction, but neither the constitution nor legislation defines the parameters. Religious instruction is optional for students. Each school defines the religious curriculum, usually in agreement with parent councils. The law prohibits public subsidies to schools that religious organizations operate.

The government observes the following religious holidays as national or regional holidays: Saint Sebastian's Day (regional), Carnaval, Ash Wednesday, Good Friday, Easter Sunday, Corpus Christi, Saint John's Day (regional), Saint George's Day(regional), Our Lady of Carmen (regional), Assumption (regional), Our Lady Aparecida, All Souls' Day, Evangelicals' Day (regional), the Feast of the Immaculate Conception (regional), and Christmas.

Government Practices

There were no reports of abuses of religious freedom.

On January 15, President Dilma Rousseff approved an agreement to include the Holocaust, anti-Semitism, and other Jewish-related subjects, as well as racism, xenophobia, and intolerance, in the curricula of some schools, universities, and other educational institutions. On August 17, following a trip by directors of five Brazilian schools named after Anne Frank, the Brazilian Jewish community announced plans to establish an educational network in which participating schools would teach tolerance according to methods the Amsterdam-based Anne Frank House educational institute developed.

On January 29, President Rousseff joined several Jewish and non-Jewish officials at a Holocaust Remembrance ceremony in Salvador to commemorate both Jewish victims and those of black African ancestry. She characterized "remembering" as a way to build the mechanisms to prevent the Holocaust from happening again, noted that the Holocaust would always stand as a paradigm against intolerance, and asserted that democratic societies had the power to fight such crimes as the Holocaust.

In July representatives of Latin America's Jewish and Arab communities met at the foreign ministry to discuss how Latin American Jews and Arabs coexist side by side harmoniously and how to export this idea of coexistence to the Middle East.

On August 5, the defense minister inaugurated a Star of David sculpture at the Monument to the Brazilian soldiers of World War II in Rio as a tribute to Jewish Brazilian soldiers who fought against Nazi fascism.

In September a judge ordered Google to remove from Brazilian YouTube versions of an amateur video many viewed as insulting to Muslims and that had sparked deadly riots across the Middle East. The ruling came in response to a National Union of Islamic Entities suit.

In Sao Paulo, municipal employees are permitted to request official time off for Yom Kippur, Rosh Hashanah, and during Ramadan.

Section III. Status of Societal Respect for Religious Freedom

There were few reports of societal discrimination based on religious affiliation, belief, or practice, and prominent societal leaders took positive steps to promote religious freedom.

In late August a Manaus city councilman published on his personal blog a photo montage of a Jewish politician's face on the body of Adolf Hitler wearing a Nazi uniform. Despite the councilman's claim that it was a "bad joke," the Israeli Committee of the Amazon, an organization of Jewish communities of the Brazilian state of Amazonas, asserted that comparing Jews to Hitler and the Nazis was anti-Semitic and offensive. The Jewish politician filed suit in the electoral court and won, but did not press civil or criminal charges. Adherents of Umbanda and Candomble reported discrimination based on religious belief. A Rio de Janeiro police officer, who heads Rio's office for investigating crimes of religious intolerance, estimated that Umbanda and Candomble followers were victims of 97 percent of religious intolerance crimes. On June 17, during the UN Summit on Sustainable Development, an estimated 2,000 Brazilians including Jews, homosexuals, Afro-Latin Americans, and human right activists protested the presence of Iranian President Mahmoud Ahmadinejad. One of the signs in English read "Religious intolerance is not acceptable." Earlier, representatives of the Brazilian Jewish community organization, the Israeli Confederation of Brazil (CONIB), urged President Rousseff not to meet with Ahmadinejad because of his repeated denials of the Holocaust, among other reasons.

There was no formal national interfaith movement; however, there were many interfaith efforts, such as Abraham's Path Initiative, an international, interfaith UN-endorsed NGO. Abraham's Path sponsored annual "friendship runs" that brought Jews, Christians, and Muslims together in an effort to increase understanding; over 4,500 persons participated in Sao Paulo.

The Commission to Combat Religious Intolerance in Rio de Janeiro, in partnership with Rio de Janeiro State University, brought together diverse religious and nonreligious groups, including Muslims, Jews, Christians, Buddhists, Spiritualists, and atheists. On September 16, the commission organized the 5th Annual Walk for the Defense of Religious Freedom held in Copacabana beach in Rio de Janeiro. At the event, various leaders spoke about the importance of religious freedom. In July an estimated 335,000 evangelical Christians participated in the 20th annual "March for Jesus" in Sao Paulo. This was the largest of many similar evangelical Christian events that took place.

The National Commission for Religious Dialogue, created in 1981 by the National Conference of Catholic Bishops, continued to bring together Christian and Jewish groups. The Catholic Church's Sao Paulo's House of Reconciliation hosted monthly meetings with the Jewish community as part of the commission's work. During the year, the House of Reconciliation initiated religious dialogues with other religions, such as Islam and Candomble.

Ecumenical movements and organizations, such as the National Council of Christian Churches, continued to bring together Catholics and Protestants. The Group of Ecumenical Reflection and Interreligious Dialogue also promoted ecumenical dialogue between different church denominations at the national and regional levels. The World Communion of Reformed Churches, World Council of Churches, and the Council for World Mission convened an ecumenical conference in Guarulhos from September 29 through October 5.

SECTION IV. U.S. GOVERNMENT POLICY

U.S. embassy officials met with many local religious leaders, continued to support the growing interfaith dialogue, and supported organizations involved in the interfaith movement, such as Abraham's Path Initiative.

In November the U.S. special representative to Muslim communities met with Muslim religious leaders in Sao Paulo and Foz de Iguacu and with students of Middle Eastern studies in Brasilia. She discussed the Hours Against Hate Initiative and opportunities for Muslim youth to promote religious tolerance through programs such as Generation Change.

In April the ambassador hosted an interfaith reception, including Jewish, Catholic, and Muslim leaders, to launch the Brazilian chapter of Generation Change, a Muslim youth-led global network to promote free exchange of ideas across borders and cultures. Subsequently, Catholic and Jewish leaders launched a similar Generation Change-inspired, youth-led initiative to integrate young people from the three religions into one group. In July, six youth leaders from Generation Change Brazil traveled to the United States as participants in a U.S. government program. They met with Muslim and interfaith groups, with American members of Generation Change, and with the Interfaith Alliance to discuss promoting tolerance and interfaith dialogue.

The U.S. embassy and consulates sponsored two U.S.-based Muslim leaders' visit to Sao Paulo and Foz do Iguacu to promote interfaith understanding. In meetings with local sheikhs and with Muslim audiences, they discussed U.S. and Brazilian experiences with religious pluralism and tolerance, and ways to promote interfaith cooperation.

In August the Sao Paulo consulate general hosted an iftar for members of the Muslim and interfaith communities. Consulate representatives participated in the September interfaith "Walk for Peace" that Abraham's Path Initiative organized.

A Recife consulate representative attended a ceremony in November marking the beginning of "Forum Dialogos," a new Pernambuco state initiative intended to foster interfaith dialogue, tolerance, and respect for freedom of religion. Many religious leaders participated in the event, including those representing Catholicism, Judaism, Anglicanism, Buddhism, Islam, spiritualism, Hare Krishnas, Tenrikyo, Candomble, and Jurema.

The principal officer in Rio de Janeiro met with the archbishop of Rio de Janeiro to discuss preparations for the 2013 World Catholic Youth Day.

In: Brazil: Conditions, Issues and U.S. Relations ISBN: 978-1-63321-253-4
Editor: Julia Sutton

Chapter 4

2013 INVESTMENT CLIMATE STATEMENT: BRAZIL*

Bureau of Economic and Business Affairs

OPENNESS TO, AND RESTRICTIONS UPON, FOREIGN INVESTMENT

Brazil is open to and encourages foreign direct investment. New foreign direct investment (FDI) into Brazil reached approximately USD 65 billion in 2012 and, according to the United Nations Conference on Trade and Development (UNCTAD) World Investment Report, Brazil is the fifth-most attractive country for FDI for the period of 2012-2014 and is consistently the largest FDI recipient in Latin America, typically receiving close to half of all South America's incoming FDI. The United States is a major foreign investor in Brazil; according to the Central Bank of Brazil, the United States had the highest stock of FDI in Brazil as of 2010, with US$104 billion. While Brazil is generally considered a friendly environment for foreign investment, complex tax and regulatory requirements exist. In most cases, these impediments apply without discrimination to both foreign and domestic firms. The Government of Brazil (GOB) generally makes no distinction between foreign and national capital in cases of direct investment.

* This is an edited, reformatted and augmented version of the Bureau of Economic and Business Affairs publication, dated February 2013.

The economy grew by around one percent in 2012, and independent analysts anticipate that it will rebound in 2013 and grow by around 3.2 percent. Medium- and long-term prospects remain favorable, supported by strong domestic demand, global demand for commodity exports, a growing middle class, expected investment in infrastructure and development of offshore oil reserves, and prudent macroeconomic policies.

Ownership Restrictions

FDI is prevalent across Brazil's economy, although certain sectors are subject to foreign ownership limitations. A 1995 constitutional amendment terminated the distinction between foreign and local capital in general, but there are laws that restrict foreign ownership within some sectors, notably aviation, insurance, and media.

Aviation

The Government of Brazil currently restricts foreign investment in domestic airline companies to a maximum of 20 percent. A bill pending in the Chamber of Deputies (PL6716) would increase that ceiling to 49 percent.

On March 19, 2011, representatives from the U.S. and Brazilian governments signed an Air Transport Agreement that will lead to an Open Skies relationship between the United States and Brazil, eliminating numerical limits on passenger and cargo flights between the two countries. If it is approved by Brazil's Congress, the agreement will take effect in October 2015. Both parties also signed a Memorandum of Consultation (MOC) that incrementally increases flight limits in the meantime. For example, in October 2012, the maximum number of weekly passenger flights was increased by 28 for U.S. airlines and by 28 for Brazilian airlines, and the maximum number of cargo flights allowed rose by 14 for each country's airlines. Additional increases will take effect in October 2013 and 2014.

Insurance

U.S. companies wanting to enter Brazil's insurance and reinsurance market must establish a subsidiary, enter into a joint venture, or acquire or partner with a local company. Market entry for banks may occur on a case-by-case basis. The Brazilian reinsurance market was opened to competition in 2007. In December 2010 and March 2011, however, the Brazilian National Council on Private Insurance (CNSP) effectively rolled back market liberalization through the issuance of Resolutions 225 and 232, which disproportionately affect foreign insurers operating in the Brazilian market. Resolution 225 requires that 40 percent of all reinsurance risk be placed with Brazilian companies. Resolution 232 allows insurance companies to place only 20 percent of risk with affiliated reinsurance companies. In December 2011, the CNSP issued Resolution 241, which walked back some of the restrictions of Resolution 225 by allowing the 40 percent requirement to be waived if local reinsurance capacity does not exist.

Media

Open broadcast (non-cable) television companies are subject to a regulation requiring that 80 percent of their programming content be domestic in origin. Foreign cable and satellite television programmers are subject to an 11 percent remittance tax; however, the tax can be avoided if the programmer invests 3 percent of its remittances in co-production of Brazilian audio-visual services. In September 2011, President Rousseff signed into force a law covering the subscription television market, including satellite and cable TV that will remove the previous 49 percent limit on foreign ownership of cable TV companies. Under the law, telecom companies will be allowed to offer television packages with their service. Content quotas will require every channel to air at least three and a half hours per week of Brazilian programming during primetime. Additionally, one-third of all channels included in any TV package will have to be Brazilian. In order to gauge public opinion regarding the telecom sector before proposing revisions to existing regulations, the Brazilian Telecommunications Agency (ANATEL) organized three public consultations in late 2011 and submitted the results to the Brazilian Congress. As a result of feedback from the Brazilian Congress, the Brazilian Supreme Court will hold further consultations in February 2013. It is anticipated that revisions to regulations could be enacted in 2013. While the results of these consultations are being considered, the previously existing law still prevails.

Foreign investment restrictions remain in a limited number of other sectors, including highway freight (20 percent) and mining of radioactive ore. Foreign ownership of land within 150 km of national borders remains prohibited unless approved by Brazil's National Security Council. In October 2009, the Chamber of Deputies approved legislation that would further restrict foreign ownership of land along Brazil's borders and within the Amazon. The proposed legislation still requires passage by the Brazilian Senate, followed by presidential approval before it can become law.

On December 9, 2011, the National Land Reform and Settlement Institute (INCRA) published a set of new rules covering the purchase of Brazilian land by foreigners.

These rules follow an August 2010 Attorney General's opinion that similarly limited foreign agricultural land ownership. Under the new rules, the area bought or leased by foreigners cannot account for more than 25 percent of the overall area in any municipal district. Additionally, no more than 10 percent of the land in any given municipal district may be owned or leased by foreign nationals from the same country. The rules also make it necessary to obtain congressional approval before large plots of land can be purchased by foreigners, foreign companies, or Brazilian companies with the majority of shareholders from foreign countries. There are several proposed bills pending in the Brazilian Congress which would clarify the process for foreigners who want to purchase land.

Infrastructure Concession

Brazil has begun an ambitious program to draw in private capital and managerial expertise to upgrade the nation's infrastructure. In February 2012, Brazil auctioned off concessions for the right to operate three of its largest airports – Juscelino Kubitschek (Brasilia), Guarulhos (Sao Paulo), and Viracopos (Campinas) – to the private sector. In December 2012, President Rousseff announced plans to auction in September 2013 additional concessions to operate the airports of Galeão (Rio de Janeiro) and Confins (Belo Horizonte).

In August 2012, government authorities announced plans to auction concessions for the right to build and operate over 6,200 miles of railroad as well as 3,500 miles of highway. Between those two projects, the Brazilian Government hopes to attract US$ 66.5 billion in private investment in roads and railroad in the next 20 years, with US$ 39.7 billion of that figure coming in the next five years.

Finally, in December 2012, President Rousseff announced plans to attract US$ 26 billion in private investment into the country's port sector within four years.

All of the infrastructure concessions are open to foreign companies. In fact, in the airport concessions, foreign companies have not only been encouraged to bid, but the auction criteria have been defined in a way that has the effect of requiring the participation of foreign airport operators. The bidding process is non-discriminatory, transparent, and performed without political interference.

Investment Goals

Between January 2011 and September 2012, the government's Program to Accelerate Growth (PAC) program disbursed US$191 billion, amounting to 40.4 percent of the spending total projected by the end of 2014. Under the program, an estimated R$959 billion was allocated for the period of 2011 through 2014. The government continues to indicate it is interested in attracting foreign investment to fund infrastructure projects.

In August 2011, Brazil announced a new industrial policy, *Plano Brasil Maior* (the "Bigger Brazil" plan), to support domestic producers, encourage investment, and spur innovation. The plan, covering the period of 2011-2014, sets targets for investment spending to reach 22.4 percent of GDP by 2014, up from a 2010 baseline of 18.4 percent. Private investment in R&D is to reach 0.90 percent of GDP by 2014, up from the 2010 figure of 0.59 percent. *Brasil Maior* also sets targets for making the economy more energy-efficient, reducing the amount of petroleum used per unit of GDP by 9 percent, and nearly tripling broadband internet penetration from 13.8 million households in 2010 to 40 million households in 2014.

The latest OECD Economic Survey for Brazil was released in 2011 and includes sections on regulatory environment, licensing, sectoral analysis, and impediments to investment. The Survey recommends continued fiscal consolidation, increased investment and savings, and additional infrastructure spending, all while incorporating the principles of social and environmental sustainability. The report can be found at: http://www.oecd.org/dataoecd/12/37/48930900.pdf.

Selected indicators from reputable third party sources

Measure	Year	Brazil Rank/Total
TI Corruption Perceptions	2012	69/176
Heritage Economic Freedom	2012	99/179
World Bank Ease of Doing Business	2013	130/185

Conversion and Transfer Policies

There are few restrictions on converting or transferring funds associated with a foreign investment in Brazil. Foreign investors may freely convert Brazilian currency in the unified foreign exchange market wherein buy-sell rates are determined by market forces. All foreign exchange transactions, including identifying data, must be reported to the Central Bank. Foreign exchange transactions on the current account have been fully liberalized.

Foreigners investing in Brazil must register their investment with the Central Bank within 30 days of the inflow of resources to Brazil. Registration is done electronically. Investments involving royalties and technology transfer must be registered with Brazil's patent office, the National Institute of Industrial Property (INPI). Investors must also have a local representative in Brazil. Portfolio investors must have a Brazilian financial administrator and register with the Brazilian Securities Exchange Commission (CVM).

All incoming foreign loans must be approved by the Central Bank. In most instances, the loans are automatically approved. Automatic approval is not issued when the costs of the loan are "not compatible with normal market conditions and practices." In such instances, the Central Bank may request additional information regarding the transaction. Foreign loans obtained abroad do not require advance approval by the Central Bank, provided the recipient is not a government entity. Loans to government entities, however, require prior approval from the Brazilian Senate as well as from the Finance Ministry Treasury Secretariat, and must be registered with the Central Bank.

Interest and amortization payments specified in a loan contract can be made without additional approval from the Central Bank. Early payments can also be made without additional approvals, if the contract includes a provision for them. Otherwise, early payment requires notification to the Central Bank to ensure accurate records of Brazil's stock of debt.

Foreign investors, upon registering their investment with the Central Bank, are able to remit dividends, capital (including capital gains), and, if applicable, royalties. Remittances must also be registered with the Central Bank. Dividends cannot exceed corporate profits. The remittance transaction may be carried out at any bank by documenting the source of the transaction (evidence of profit or sale of assets) and showing that applicable taxes have been paid.

Capital gain remittances are subject to a 15 percent income withholding tax, with the exception of the capital gains and interest payments on tax-exempt domestically issued Brazilian bonds. Repatriation of the initial investment is also exempt from income tax. Lease payments are assessed a 15 percent withholding tax.

Remittances related to technology transfers are not subject to the tax on credit, foreign exchange, and insurance, although they are subject to a 15 percent withholding tax and an extra 10 percent Contribution of Intervention in the Economic Domain (CIDE).

The Government of Brazil imposes the IOF, a tax on financial operations, on portfolio capital inflows. The main goal of the tax is to discourage short-term, speculative capital flows that could lead to excessive currency volatility or significant appreciation pressures on the Brazilian currency. The GOB made several tweaks to the IOF over the course of 2012 based on changes in the size and pace of portfolio inflows into Brazil and developments in international financial markets. The IOF ended the year at 6.0 percent of all foreign loans with terms of 720 days or less used to fund operations in Brazil. Those with a longer maturity are exempt. Profits and FDI remittances must pay an IOF of 0.38 percent.

Expropriation and Compensation

There have been no expropriation actions in Brazil against foreign interests in the recent past, nor have there been any signs that the current government is contemplating such actions. In the past, some claims regarding land expropriations by state agencies have been judged by courts in U.S. citizens' favor. However, compensation has not always been paid as states have filed appeals to these decisions, and the Brazilian judicial system moves slowly.

Dispute Settlement

The Brazilian court system, in general, is overburdened, and contract disputes can be lengthy and complex. The 2013 World Bank "Doing Business" survey found that on average it takes 44 procedures and 731 days to litigate a contract breach at an average cost of 16.5 percent of the claim.

Article 34 of Brazilian Law 9,307, the 1996 Brazilian Arbitration Act, defines a foreign arbitration judgment as any judgment rendered outside the national territory. The law established that the Brazilian Federal Supreme Court must ratify foreign arbitration awards. Law 9,307 also stipulates that the foreign arbitration award is to be recognized or executed in Brazil in conformity with the international agreements ratified by the country and, in their absence, with domestic law. (Note: A 2001 Federal Supreme Court ruling established that the 1996 Brazilian Arbitration Act, permitting international arbitration subject to Federal Supreme Court ratification of arbitration decisions, does not violate the Federal Constitution's provision that "the law shall not exclude any injury or threat to a right from the consideration of the Judicial Power.")

Brazil has ratified the 1975 Inter-American Convention on International Commercial Arbitration (Panama Convention), the 1979 Inter-American Convention on Extraterritorial Validity of Foreign Judgments and Arbitration Awards (Montevideo Convention) and the 1958 U.N. Convention on the Recognition and Enforcement of Foreign Arbitration Awards (New York Convention). Brazil, however, is not a member of the International Center for the Settlement of Investment Disputes (ICSID), also known as the Washington Convention.

Brazil has a commercial code that governs most aspects of commercial association, except for corporations formed for the provision of professional services, which are governed by the civil code. In 2005, bankruptcy legislation (Law 11101) went into effect creating a system, modeled on Chapter 11 of the U.S. bankruptcy code, which allows a company in financial trouble to negotiate a restructuring with its creditors outside of the courts. In the event a company does fail despite restructuring efforts, the reforms give creditors improved ability to recover their debts.

Brazil has both a federal and a state court system, and jurisprudence is based on civil law. Federal judges hear most disputes in which one of the parties is the State and rule on lawsuits between a foreign State or international organization and a municipality or a person residing in Brazil. Five regional federal courts hear appeals of federal judges' decisions.

Performance Requirements and Incentives

The Brazilian government uses a variety of tax incentives and attractive financing through the National Bank for Economic and Social Development (BNDES) to actively encourage both domestic and foreign investment. In 2012, BNDES disbursements rose 12 percent to reach R$156 billion, making it the largest development bank in the world, outpacing the lending of even the World Bank. BNDES funding in 2012 was focused on industry and infrastructure, with R$18.9 billion for the electricity sector, R$15.5 billion for transportation, and R$8.5 billion for chemicals and petrochemicals. BNDES also actively promotes development in traditionally underserved populations and regions of the country and in other potentially less profitable ventures, but the majority of lending takes place in the more industrialized regions of the country. A 2004 Public-Private Partnership (PPP) investment law promotes joint ventures in otherwise marginally profitable infrastructure investments.

The Government of Brazil extends tax benefits for investment in less developed parts of the country, for example the Northeast and the Amazon regions, with equal application to foreign and domestic investors. These incentives have been successful in attracting major foreign plants to areas like the Manaus Free Trade Zone, but most foreign investment remains concentrated in the more industrialized southern part of Brazil.

Individual states have sought to attract investment by offering ad hoc tax benefits and infrastructure support to specific companies, negotiated on a case by case basis. These benefits have spurred a so-called "fiscal war" between the states, with some states challenging the tax benefits as harmful fiscal competition. In June 2011, the Brazilian Supreme Court ruled that the benefits granted by 14 states on interstate commerce are unconstitutional, as they were implemented without unanimous consent from the National Council of Fiscal Policy (Confaz). In November 2012, the Ministry of Finance proposed to Congress an end to the "fiscal war" by setting the interstate tax rate on goods at 4 percent for all states, thus limiting states' ability to offer special tax incentives to attract investment away from other states. A decision on this proposal by Congress is expected in early 2013, but previous attempts at interstate tax reform have failed to gain Congressional support.

In October 2012, the GOB announced Decree 7819 in support of domestic auto manufacturers. The decree raised the Industrial Products Tax (IPI) by 30 percentage points of the price of the vehicle on all vehicle sales in the Brazilian market on or after January 1, 2013. This change affected all vehicles: domestically-produced, imports from other Mercosur member countries, imports from Mexico within quota, and all other foreign imports. Auto manufacturers are able to apply for a tax credit based on their ability to meet certain criteria, including the number of manufacturing processes performed in Brazil, enhancing fuel efficiency, committing to research and development investment in Brazil or Brazilian engineering services, and agreeing to participate in a fuel-efficiency labeling scheme. This decree is the successor to the September 2011 decree (No. 7567) which called for a 30 percentage point increase in the IPI on any car not sourced with at least 65 percent of parts from Merciful countries or Mexico, with which Brazil has an auto sector trade agreement. Decree 7567 expired on December 31, 2012. Both decrees are clear moves to encourage manufacturers to produce in Brazil rather than exporting cars to Brazil.

In December 2011, the Government of Brazil passed Law 12546, which introduced the Special Regime for the Reinstatement of Taxes for Exporters, dubbed the Reintegra Program. Exporters of products covering 8,630 tariff codes – representing R$80 billion of exports – will receive a subsidy of 3 percent of the value of their exports, to be used either as a credit against their income tax or as a cash payment. To qualify, the imported content of the exported goods must not exceed 40%, except in the case of high-tech goods, such as pharmaceuticals, electronics, and aircraft and parts, which are permitted to have up to 65% of inputs imported. In addition, Reintegra exempts exporters from so-called indirect taxes on capital expenditures, including the PIS/Cofins social contribution taxes and the IOF tax on financial transactions. The Reintegra Program, originally scheduled to expire at the end of 2012, was extended by the Ministry of Finance until December 31, 2013.

In December 2011, as part of the Plano Brasil Maior, the government of Brazil approved a corporate payroll tax exemption to businesses within the sectors of industry, trade and services. The measure originally ordered the exemption of payroll taxes for companies within the information technology, textile, leather and footwear sectors. At the end of 2012, the payroll exemption was extended to a total of 42 sectors to include construction metals, big appliances and pharmaceutical products for example. The measure replaced the 20 percent payroll tax for social security contributions with a rate between 1 and 2 percent of company gross operating revenue (less export revenue).

In May of 2010, the government placed state-owned communications firm Telebras at the head of a National Broadband Plan which incorporates fiscal incentives, private sector participation, and regulatory reform to build out Brazil's next generation communication infrastructure network. While the plan provides commercial opportunities for the private sector, including foreign investors, the government seeks to leverage the plan to advance Brazilian technology. This includes favorable BNDES financing for acquisition of telecom equipment that utilizes Brazilian technology, tax exemptions on the purchase of IT equipment that uses Brazilian technology, as well as favoring domestic technology in the procurement process.

As of October 2011, internet companies in Brazil began to offer broadband for as low as R$35.00 (US$19) per month. The "Internet for the People" initiative, part of the National Broadband Plan, aims to bring high-speed connections to 40 million homes, part of the government's efforts to increase digital inclusion throughout Brazilian society. The GOB seeks to connect all Brazilian municipalities to the internet no later than 2014. In addition to cutting the price of internet connections in half, the Brazilian government will provide free internet access to 59,000 public elementary and high schools. In the most marginal communities including rural settlements and indigenous communities, the Ministry of Communication will establish 13,000 Telecenters to boost digital inclusion.

To promote Brazilian industry, the Special Agency for Industrial Financing (FINAME) of BNDES provides financing for Brazilian firms to purchase Brazilian-made machinery and equipment and capital goods with a high level of domestic content. The interest rates charged by BNDES are often significantly lower than the prevailing market interest rates for domestic financing.

Government Procurement

Brazil is not a signatory to the WTO Agreement on Government Procurement (GPA). U.S. companies seeking to participate in Brazil's public sector procurement effectively need to partner with a local firm or have operations in Brazil. Foreign companies are often successful in obtaining subcontracting opportunities with large Brazilian firms that win government contracts.

Law 8666 (1993) covers most government procurement other than information technology/telecommunications and requires non-discriminatory treatment for all bidders regardless of nationality or origin of the product or service. Brazilian government procurement rules apply to purchases by government entities and state-owned companies. Brazil has an open competition process for major government procurements. The Brazilian government may not make a distinction between domestic and foreign-owned companies during the tendering process; however, when two equally qualified vendors are considered, the law's implementing regulations provide for a preference to Brazilian goods and services. Price is to be the overriding factor in selecting suppliers (see update in the following paragraph). However, the law's implementing regulations also allow for the consideration of non-price factors, giving preferences to certain goods produced in Brazil and stipulating local content requirements for fiscal benefits eligibility. Additionally, nearly all bids require establishment of a local representative for any foreign company bidding.

Brazil continued to apply preference margins to government procurement in 2012. In 2010, then-President Lula signed a decree that later was approved by the Congress and became law (No. 12,349, December 15, 2010), giving preference to firms that produce in Brazil -- whether foreign-owned or Brazilian -- that fulfill certain economic stimulus requirements such as generating employment or contributing to technological development, even when their bids are up to 25 percent more expensive than competing imported products. In August 2011, this system of preference margins was folded into Plano Brasil Maior. Government procurement is just one of thirty-five components under Brasil Maior intended to support Brazilian industry and protect domestic producers, particularly the labor-intensive sectors threatened by imports. The textile, clothing and footwear industries – among the few industries to have lost jobs during the current growth period – were the first to benefit from Brasil Maior when, in November 2011, the Ministry of Development, Industry and Commerce implemented an 8 percent preference margin for domestic producers in these industries when bidding on government contracts. In April 2012, Decrees 7709 and 7713 expanded the use of preference margins to pharmaceuticals and medicine (8 or 20 percent) and excavators and bulldozers (15 and 25 percent).

Decree 7174 (2010), which regulates the procurement of information technology goods and services, requires federal agencies and parastatal entities to give preferential treatment to domestically produced computer products and goods or services with technology developed in Brazil based on a complicated price/technology matrix.

Right to Private Ownership and Establishment

Foreign and domestic private entities may establish, own, and dispose of business enterprises.

Protection of Property Rights

Mortgages

Brazil has a system in place for mortgage registration, but implementation is uneven and there is no standardized contract. Foreign individuals or foreign-owned companies can purchase real property in Brazil. These buyers frequently arrange alternative financing in their own countries, where rates may be more attractive. Law 9514 (1997) helped spur the mortgage industry by establishing a legal framework for a secondary market in mortgages and streamlining the foreclosure process, but the mortgage market in Brazil is still underdeveloped, and foreigners may have difficulty obtaining mortgage financing. Large U.S. real estate firms, nonetheless, are expanding their portfolios in Brazil.

Intellectual Property Rights

Brazil is a signatory to the GATT Uruguay Round Agreements, including the Trade Related Aspects of Intellectual Property (TRIPs) Agreement, which it signed in 1994. Brazil is a signatory of the Bern Convention on Artistic Property, the Patent Cooperation Treaty, the Convention on Plant Variety Protection, and the Paris Convention on Protection of Intellectual Property.

Brazil is not a party to the WIPO Copyright Treaty or the WIPO Performances and Phonograms Treaty (collectively, the "WIPO Internet Treaties"). In 2006, Brazil announced plans to join the Madrid Agreement Concerning the International Registration of Marks ("Madrid Protocol"), but the executive branch has yet to submit this proposal to the Brazilian Congress for approval.

In most respects, Brazil's 1996 Industrial Property Law (Law 9279) meets the international standards specified in the TRIPs Agreement regarding patent and trademark protection. However, the law permits the grant of a compulsory license if a patent owner has failed to locally manufacture the patented invention in Brazil within three years of patent issuance, a form of compulsory licensing that the United States believes would be inconsistent with Articles 27.1 and 28.1 of TRIPs. On May 4, 2007, invoking TRIPS provisions for public health emergencies, Brazil issued a compulsory license for an anti-retroviral drug used in treating HIV/AIDS.

The United States continues to raise concerns regarding article 229-C of law 9279, as amended by Law 10196 (2001), which includes a requirement for the National Health Surveillance Agency (ANVISA) to grant an approval prior to the issuance of a pharmaceutical patent by the National Industrial Property Institute (INPI). Due to ANVISA's role in reviewing pharmaceutical patent applications – known as "prior consent" – there is a significant backlog in the issuance of patents. In addition, conflicting opinions on patentability between INPI and ANVISA have left more than 140 patent applications unissued. On October 16, 2009, the Brazilian Federal Attorney General (AGU), analyzing the institutional role of ANVISA in the patent application process, presented Opinion No. 210, which stated that ANVISA should examine pharmaceutical patent applications only from a public health perspective. The opinion states that INPI is the only agency with the competency to review the patentability requirements of such applications. On January 10, 2011, the AGU issued another opinion noting ANVISA's limited role, saying "ANVISA may not refuse the granting of the prior consent of art. 229-C of IP Law based on patentability requirements." The AGU´s opinions were not binding, and the Brazilian Federal Government created an Inter-Ministerial working group to study how to best implement the AGU's opinions.

On May 24, 2012, Inter-Ministerial Ruling no. 1056 was published, reporting the outcome of the working group. According to the ruling, all patent applications claiming pharmaceutical products and/or processes are to be initially analysed by ANVISA. If ANVISA grants its approval, then it will be assessed by the INPI. No other industrial sector is treated in this way. For all other patent applications, INPI is the sole arbiter of whether or not a patent is granted, and other agencies regulate market access.

On October 17, 2012, ANVISA opened public consultations on its proposed new regulations for prior consent. The new regulations reverse the existing workflow of pharmaceutical patent applications, as suggested by Ruling no. 1056. They also permit ANVISA´s analyses of patent applications to go beyond a public health perspective, to include patentability standards that are traditionally the domain of patent offices worldwide. The deadline to comment on the new regulations was December 20, 2012. It is unclear when the proposed regulations will be promulgated. The final result may have an effect on both product availability and capital inflows for the sector. If the system as currently proposed goes forward it may diminish the likelihood that newer "on patent" medications will be produced or even sold in Brazil.

An additional ongoing concern is the backlog of pending patent applications at INPI. INPI claims it takes an average of five years to receive a patent in Brazil; independent resources, however, state that it takes six to seven years. INPI has increased its hiring and training of new patent examiners in an effort to decrease pendency. In March 2013, INPI plans to begin rolling out an electronic filing system for new patent applications, which would enable inventors to file a patent application using an online system.

The United States has also raised concerns regarding Brazil's protection against unfair commercial use of test data generated in connection with obtaining marketing approval for human-use pharmaceutical products. Law 10603 (2002) covers data confidentiality for veterinary pharmaceuticals, fertilizers, agro-toxins, and related products, but does not cover pharmaceuticals for human use, which potentially inhibits the introduction of certain products into the market since a generic manufacturer can produce a copy locally and rely upon the safety and efficacy data of the originator.

A Brazilian government-drafted bill to provide protection for the layout design of integrated circuits (computer mask works) was enacted into law on May 31, 2007 (Law 11.484).

Patent and trademark licensing agreements must be recorded with and approved by INPI and registered with the Central Bank of Brazil (Normative Act No. 135, of April 15, 1997). Licensing contracts must contain detailed information about the terms of the agreement and royalties to be paid. In such arrangements, Brazilian law limits the amount of the royalty payment that can be taken as a tax deduction (from one percent to five percent), which consequently acts as a de facto cap on licensing fees (Act No. 436 of 1958).

Brazil's 1998 copyright law generally conforms to international standards, yet piracy of copyrighted material remains a problem. The Brazilian Congress passed a law in July 2003 increasing minimum prison sentences for copyright violations and establishing procedures for making arrests and the destruction of confiscated products. Draft Law 333 of 1999 would stiffen the criminal penalties for counterfeiting, but it remains stalled in the Brazilian Congress. After being shelved in 2006, the draft law was re-submitted in November 2008 for urgent reconsideration, but the proposal has still not come to a vote.

In August 2007, a bill (PL 1807/07) was introduced that, if approved, would amend Article 189 of Brazil's Industrial Property Law (Law 9279 of 1996) to increase the criminal penalties for trademark violations to two to six years, up from the current three to twelve months. The bill was approved by the House and sent to the Senate in June 2012, where it is currently being analyzed.

In the U.S. Trade Representative's 2007 Special 301 Report, Brazil was downgraded from "Priority Watch List" to "Watch List," in recognition of its improved anti-piracy enforcement efforts. Since then, Brazil has remained on the "Watch List" of the Special 301 Reports. Anti-piracy enforcement has continued to improve, especially in the major cities of Sao Paulo, Rio de Janeiro, and Brasilia. The upcoming 2014 FIFA soccer World Cup and 2016 Olympics will continue to drive this trend of strong anti-piracy and anti-counterfeiting efforts by local, state, and federal police.

Transparency of the Regulatory System

In the 2013 World Bank 'Doing Business' report, Brazil ranked 130th out of 185 countries in terms of overall ease of doing business, a decline of four places versus the 2012 report. According to the study, it takes an average of 13 procedures and 119 days to start a new business, significantly longer than the OECD high-income economies' average of 11.8 days. The study noted that the annual administrative burden to a medium-size business of tax payments in Brazil is an average of 2,600 hours versus 176 hours in the OECD high-income economies. According to this same study, the total tax rate for Brazil's medium-sized business is 69.3 percent of profits, compared to 42.7 percent in the OECD high-income economies. Business managers often complain of not understanding tax regulations, despite best efforts including large tax and accounting departments.

Tax regulations, while burdensome and numerous, do not differentiate between foreign and domestic firms. However, there have been instances of complaints that the value-added tax collected by individual states (ICMS) favors local companies. Although the tax is designed to be refunded upon export of goods outside of the country, exporters in many states have had difficulty receiving their ICMS rebates. Taxes on commercial and financial transactions are particularly burdensome, and businesses complain that these taxes hinder the international competitiveness of Brazilian-made products.

Of Brazil's ten federal regulatory agencies, the most prominent include ANVISA, the Brazilian FDA equivalent having regulatory authority over the production and marketing of food, drugs and medical devices; ANATEL, the country's telecommunication agency handling licensing and assigning bandwidth, ANP, the National Petroleum Agency regulating oil and gas contracts and overseeing the bidding process to acquire oil blocks, including for pre-salt oil; and ANAC, the agency overseeing the civil aviation industry. In addition to these federal regulatory agencies, Brazil has 23 state-level agencies and eight municipal-level agencies. Despite the existence of these bodies, the lack of a formal, federal-level institution tasked with coordinating the regulatory framework can often complicate Brazil's regulatory process.

The Office of the Presidency's Program for the Strengthening of Institutional Capacity for Management in Regulation (PRO-REG), created in 2007, has tried to introduce a broad program for improving the regulatory framework in Brazil, but lacks the authority to act as a single coordinating agency.

Pursuant to the Rousseff administration's priority to improve transparency, the general public has online access to both approved and proposed federal legislation, via websites for the Chamber of Deputies, Federal Senate, and the Office of the Presidency. While there is currently no system in place for public comment on these proposed laws and regulations,

this has been identified by the Brazilian government as a key priority in improving Brazil's regulatory system.

Foreign investors have encountered obstacles when interfacing with regulatory agencies. Notable examples include companies in the electric power sector that have complained about the high level of regulatory risk, including the tariff review process. Additionally, some industries have reported challenges in obtaining licenses from IBAMA, the environmental regulator; citing unpredictability in IBAMA's licensing requirements, though the process has reportedly become more streamlined since 2008. There have also been examples of federal agencies levying significant fines on U.S. companies. In October 2011, Brazilian private insurance regulator (SUSEP) announced its intention to fine U.S. insurance company National Western Life US$ 6 billion for selling insurance contracts without being licensed in Brazil. The fine, which would be the largest in the history of Brazil's financial system, was upheld by SUSEP in mid-2012 and is currently under appeal. In 2012, various Brazilian regulatory agencies including IBAMA, Brazil's National Petroleum Agency (ANP), and the Rio de Janeiro State Institute of Environment (INEA) imposed separate fines on Chevron for damages related to a November 2011 offshore oil seep from near a Chevron-operated well; the ANP fines were eventually reduced to US$ 12 million and was paid by Chevron in September 2012. As of January, 2013, regulators had not yet granted Chevron approval to resume operations. Brazilian private sector organizations, which often include foreign companies, are vocal and involved in industry standards setting.

Regulatory review of mergers and acquisitions are carried out by the Administrative Council for Economic Defense (CADE). In October 2012, Brazil performed its first-ever pre-merger review of a pending merger, bringing Brazil in line with U.S. and European practices. Brazil had previously performed only post-merger reviews. This shift in merger review was a result of 2011 legislation (law 12,529) which was adopted to modernize Brazil's antitrust review and to combine the antitrust functions of the Ministry of Justice and the Ministry of Finance into those of the so-called Super CADE. This new government body will be responsible for enforcement of competition laws, consumer defense, and combating abuse of economic power.

Efficient Capital Markets and Portfolio Investment

The Brazilian financial sector is large and sophisticated. Banks lend at Brazilian market rates which, while they have fallen since 2011, remains high.

Reasons cited by industry observers include high taxation, repayment risk, concern over inconsistent judicial enforcement of contracts, high mandatory reserve requirements, and administrative overhead.

The financial sector is concentrated, with 2012 Central Bank data indicating that the 10 largest commercial banking institutions account for approximately 81 percent of financial sector assets, less brokerages (approx. US$ 2 trillion). Three of the five largest banks (in assets) in the country, Banco do Brasil, Caixa Economica Federal, and BNDES, are partially or completely federally owned. Lending by the large banking institutions is focused on the largest companies, while small and medium banks primarily serve small and medium-sized companies, but with a much smaller capital base.

The Central Bank has strengthened bank audits, implemented more stringent internal control requirements, and tightened capital adequacy rules to better reflect risk. It also established loan classification and provisioning requirements. These measures are applied to private and publicly owned banks alike. The Brazilian Securities and Exchange Commission (CVM) independently regulate the stock exchanges, brokers, distributors, pension funds, mutual funds, and leasing companies with penalties against insider trading.

Credit Market

Brazil's credit market has grown significantly over the past several years. Real interest rates, once among the highest in the world, fell dramatically in 2012, driven by continued decreases in the Central Bank's benchmark overnight Selic lending rate and a concerted effort by the GOB to reduce lending spreads charged by public and private banks. While local private sector banks are beginning to offer longer credit terms, BNDES, the government national development bank, is the traditional Brazilian source of longer-term credit, and also provides export credits. FINAME (the Special Agency for Industrial Financing) provides foreign and domestically owned companies operating in Brazil financing for the manufacturing and marketing of capital goods. FINAMEX (Export Financing), which finances capital good exports for both foreign and domestic companies, is a part of FINAME. One of the goals of these financing options is to support the purchase of domestically produced over imported equipment and machinery.

Equity Market

All stock trading is performed on the Sao Paulo Stock Exchange (BOVESPA), while trading of public securities is conducted on the Rio de

Janeiro market. In 2008, the Brazilian Mercantile & Futures Exchange (BM&F) merged with the BOVESPA to form what is now the fourth largest exchange in the Western Hemisphere, after the NYSE, NASDAQ, and Canadian TSX Group exchanges. BOVESPA has launched a "New Market," in which the listed companies comply with stricter corporate governance requirements. A majority of Initial Public Offerings are now listed on the New Market. In 2012, twelve new IPOs and follow-ons raised R$ 13 billion in capital; approximately 36 percent of this amount was foreign capital.

At the end of 2012, there were 452 companies traded on the BM&F/BOVESPA. Total daily trading average volume has risen from R$ 2.4 billion in 2006 to R$ 7.2 billion in 2012, and the number of trades has increased more than 10 times over the same period.

The BM&F/BOVESPA currently has no competition, but that may change soon. In January 2013, Direct Edge, the fourth-largest stock exchange operator in the United States, announced that it would shortly apply for a license to launch its services in Brazil in 2013. If the plan is approved by Brazil regulators, Direct Edge will serve as an alternative trading platform to the BOVESPA. Foreign investors, both institutions and individuals, can directly invest in equities, securities and derivatives. Foreign investors are required to trade derivatives and stocks of publicly held companies on established markets. At year-end 2012, foreign investors accounted for 40.3 percent of the total turnover on the BOVESPA. Domestic institutional investors were the second most active market participants, accounting for 32 percent of activity. Individual investors comprised 17.9 percent of activity, followed by financial institutions (8.1 percent), and public and private companies (1.9 percent). Law 10303 of 2001 limits preferred shares to 50 percent of new issuances.

Wholly owned subsidiaries of multinational accounting firms, including the major U.S. firms, are present in Brazil. As of 1996, auditors are personally liable for the accuracy of accounting statements prepared for banks.

In recent years the government has sought to manage short-term capital inflows and appreciation of the Brazilian currency with the introduction of new taxes on capital inflows (see “Conversion and Transfer Policies” section above).

Competition from State-Owned Enterprises

In the 1990’s and early 2000s, the Brazilian government privatized state enterprises across a broad spectrum of industries, including mining, steel, aeronautics, banking, energy, and electricity generation and distribution. While the government has divested itself from many of its state-owned companies, it maintains partial control (at both the federal and state level) of some previously wholly state-owned enterprises. Notable examples of partially federally-controlled firms include energy giant Petrobras and power utility Eletrobras. Both Petrobras and Eletrobras include non-government shareholders, are listed on both the Brazilian and NYSE stock exchanges, and are subject to the same accounting and audit regulations as all publicly traded Brazilian companies.

The 2010 pre-salt legislation gives Petrobras sole operator status for the development of the new oil discoveries. The terms and conditions of the new regime favor Petrobras as the sole operator, although foreign firms are still anticipated to play a role in the pre-salt oil fields.

In addition to major players like Petrobras and Eletrobras, the Brazilian government, at both the federal and state levels, maintains ownership interests in a variety of other smaller enterprises. Typically, corporate governance is led by a board comprised of directors elected by the state or federal government with additional directors elected by non-government shareholders. Brazilian enterprises with state ownership are concentrated in the energy, electricity generation and distribution, transportation, and banking sectors. Many of these firms are also publically traded companies on the Brazilian and other stock exchanges.

The GOB created a number of new state-owned enterprises in 2012. In August, the Planning and Logistics Company (EPL) was founded to oversee the development and integration of various forms of transportation, including the concessions for roads and railways. The EPL is also responsible for the development of the bullet train project that will connect Sao Paulo, Campinas, and Rio de Janeiro.

Also in August, President Rousseff signed a provisional measure (MP 564) which would allow for the creation of a state-owned enterprise for reinsurance, the Brazilian Management Agency of Funds and Guarantees, known as "Segurobras." The purpose of the company would be to provide government-backed reinsurance for large infrastructure projects, such as for World Cup and Olympics construction, which do not have full coverage in the private market.

In December, the GOB created Infraero Serviços, a state-owned company mandated to manage the network of regional airports. The GOB intends for Infraero Serviços to eventually co-manage the airports along with a private sector concessionaire.

Corporate Social Responsibility

Most state-owned and private sector corporations of any significant size in Brazil pursue corporate social responsibility (CSR) activities. Many corporations support local education, health and other programs in the communities where they have a presence. Brazilian consumers, especially the local citizenry where a corporation has or is planning a local presence, expect CSR activity. It is not uncommon for corporate officials to meet with community members prior to building a new plant or factory to review what types of local services the corporation will commit to providing. Foreign and local enterprises in Brazil often advance United Nations Development Program (UNDP) Millennium Development Goals (MDGs) as part of their CSR activity, and will cite their local contributions to MDGs such as universal primary education and environmental sustainability.

The U.S. diplomatic mission in Brazil supports American business CSR activities through the +Unidos Group (Mais Unidos), a group of more than 100 American companies established in Brazil. Additional information on how the partnership supports public and private alliances in Brazil can be found on its website: www.maisunidos.org.

The private sector in Brazil is increasingly engaging in public-private partnerships for investments in environmental and socio-economic development initiatives. Currently Mais Unidos, in partnership with USAID, has two joint projects in the areas of education and environment. The education/English language project, Mais Opportunidades, has been operating in Rio de Janeiro since 2011 with the support from the Rio de Janeiro state government, and will benefit disadvantaged youth. The environment project, Mais Unidos for the Amazon, contributes to preserve the biodiversity of the region.

Political Violence

Strikes and demonstrations occur occasionally in urban areas and may cause temporary disruption to public transportation. Widespread public sector strikes by federal government employees in Brasilia in 2012 remained peaceful. Although U.S. citizens have traditionally not been targeted during such events, U.S. citizens traveling or residing in Brazil are advised to take common-sense precautions and avoid any large gatherings or any other event where crowds have congregated to demonstrate or protest. For the latest U.S.

State Department guidance on travel in Brazil, please consult www.travel.state.gov.

Corruption

In 2012, Brazil ranked 69th (out of 174 countries) in Transparency International's Corruption Perceptions Index. In South America, Brazil ranked behind Chile and Uruguay, and ranked ahead of Colombia, Peru, Argentina, Suriname, Bolivia, Ecuador, Guyana, Paraguay and Venezuela. With regard to major emerging economies in the BRICS grouping, Brazil ranked ahead of China (80th), India (94th), and Russia (133rd), and tied with South Africa (69th).

Corruption scandals are a regular feature of Brazilian political life. Politics in 2012 were dominated by Penal Case 470, more commonly known as the "Mensalão" case, under which defendants including some past and present members of the Brazilian Congress were found guilty of participating in a pay-for-votes scheme. A former president of the Chamber of Deputies, former President Lula's chief of staff, and 24 other current and former public officials were convicted in the highly-followed trial, which was viewed as a positive step in the fight against corruption. In her first year in office, 2011, President Rousseff dismissed six ministers after allegations of diversion of public funds and/or influence peddling in their ministries. Authorities have conducted corruption investigations involving politicians from both opposition and government coalition parties over the course of the last several years.

Brazil is a signatory to the Organization for Economic Cooperation and Development (OECD) Anti-Bribery Convention. It was one of the founders, along with the United States, of the intergovernmental Open Government Partnership, which seeks to help governments increase transparency. Brazil has laws, regulations and penalties to combat corruption, but their effectiveness is inconsistent. Bribery is illegal, and a bribe by a local company to a foreign official is a criminal act. A company cannot deduct a bribe to a foreign official from its taxes. While federal government authorities generally investigate allegations of corruption, there are inconsistencies in the level of enforcement among individual states. Corruption has been reported to be problematic in business dealings with some authorities, particularly at the municipal level. U.S. companies operating in Brazil are subject to the U.S. Foreign Corrupt Practices Act.

Bilateral Investment Agreements

Brazil does not have a Bilateral Investment Treaty with the United States. In the 1990's Brazil signed BITs with Belgium and Luxembourg, Chile, Cuba, Denmark, Finland, France, Germany, Italy, the Republic of Korea, the Netherlands, Portugal, Switzerland, the United Kingdom and Venezuela, but none of these have been approved by the Brazilian Congress. Brazil also has not approved the Mercosur investment protocol.

Brazil does not have a double taxation treaty with the United States, but it does have such treaties with 24 other countries, including, among others, Japan, France, Italy, the Netherlands, Canada and Argentina. Brazil signed a Tax Information Exchange Agreement with the United States in March 2007 that passed the Brazilian Chamber of Deputies in December 2009 and currently awaits action in the Brazilian Senate.

OPIC and Other Investment Insurance Programs

Programs of the Overseas Private Investment Corporation (OPIC) are fully available, and activity has increased in recent years. The size of OPIC's exposure in Brazil may occasionally limit its capacity for new coverage. Brazil has been a member of the Multilateral Investment Guarantee Agency (MIGA) since 1992.

Labor

The Brazilian Ministry of Finance estimates that 19.3 million jobs were created in Brazil from January 2003 to October 2012. In 2012, a net 1.3 million jobs were created, compared to 1.9 million in 2011.

According to a 2011 Brazilian Institute of Geography and Statistics (IBGE) report, the Brazilian labor force is 92.5 million workers strong. Roughly 58% were located in the services sector, 15% in agriculture, 21% in the construction and manufacturing.

Brazil has signed on to a large number of International Labor Organization (ILO) conventions. Brazil is party to the U.N. Convention on the Rights of the Child and major ILO conventions concerning the prohibition of child labor, forced labor and discrimination.

The labor code is highly detailed and relatively generous to workers. Formal sector workers are guaranteed 30 days of annual leave and severance pay in the case of dismissal without cause. Brazilian employers are required to pay a "thirteenth month" of salary to employees at the end of the year. Brazil also has a system of labor courts that are charged with resolving routine cases involving unfair dismissal, working conditions, salary disputes, and other grievances. Labor courts have the power to impose an agreement on employers and unions if negotiations break down and either side appeals to the court system. As a result, labor courts routinely are called upon to determine wages and working conditions in industries across the country. The system is tantamount to compulsory arbitration and does not encourage collective bargaining. In recent years, however, both labor and management have become more flexible and collective bargaining has assumed greater relevance.

The Ministry of Labor estimates that there are nearly 15,000 labor unions in Brazil, but Ministry officials note that these figures are inexact. Labor unions, especially in sectors such as metalworking and banking, tend to be well-organized and aggressive in advocating for wages and working conditions and account for approximately 19 percent of the official workforce according to a recent IBGE release. Strikes occur periodically, particularly among public sector unions. Unions in various sectors engage in industry-wide collective bargaining negotiations mandated by federal regulation. While some labor organizations and their leadership operate independently of the government and of political parties, others are viewed as closely associated with political parties.

In firms employing three or more persons, Brazilian nationals must constitute at least two-thirds of all employees and receive at least two-thirds of total payroll. Foreign specialists in fields where Brazilians are unavailable are not counted in calculating the one-third permitted for non-Brazilians.

The IBGE statistical agency estimated unemployment in the major metropolitan areas as of December 2012 at 4.6 percent. With low unemployment, there is currently a shortage of highly-skilled workers. Unemployment levels range significantly across regions.

IBGE reports show that real wages have trended higher in recent years. The average monthly wage in Brazil's six largest cities was around R$1,787.70 in October 2012 (approximately USD 880 based on average exchange rates for that month). The minimum monthly wage has regularly been increased in recent years from R$380 in 2007 to R$671 (approximately USD 335) in 2013. Earnings vary significantly by region and industry, and there is significant, though gradually declining, income inequality between Brazil's poor and wealthy.

Employer federations, supported by mandatory fees based on payroll, play a significant role in both public policy and labor relations. Each state has its own federation, which reports to the National Confederation of Industries (CNI), headquartered in Brasilia.

Foreign Trade Zones/Free Trade Zones

The federal government has granted tax benefits for certain free trade zones. Most of these free trade zones aim to attract investment to the country's relatively underdeveloped North and Northeast regions. The most prominent of these is the Manaus Free Trade Zone, in Amazonas State, which has attracted significant foreign investment, including from U.S. companies. According to SUFRAMA, the Brazilian federal agency responsible for the economic development of the Amazon region, for the eleven months ending November 2012, the companies of the Manaus industrial area generated USD 32.8 billion in revenues, an increase of 22.6 percent over the same period in 2011. In October 2011, President Rousseff signed a constitutional amendment which extends Manaus's status as an industrial zone for another 50 years.

Foreign Direct Investment and Foreign Direct Investment Statistics

According to the Central Bank's most recent foreign-capital census (2010), the United States had the largest share of accumulated foreign-capital stock in Brazil, with 18.0 percent of the total. Spain had 14.7 percent, Belgium 8.7 percent, and Brazil 8.3 percent. Net foreign direct investment inflows between the years 2006 to 2011 have amounted to about USD 377 billion, after subtracting depreciation and capital repatriation.

According to the UN, Brazil was in 2012 the fourth largest destination of foreign direct investment, trailing only the United States, China, and Hong Kong. The same criteria placed Brazil in fifth in 2011 and seventh in 2010.

According to data published by the Central Bank, FDI inflows to Brazil are anticipated to have reached more than USD 65 billion in 2012, a figure 2 percent lower than 2011. Additionally, according to the U.S. Bureau of

Economic Analysis, the stock of FDI from the United States in Brazil was USD 71.1 billion as of the end of 2011.

Total FDI flows into Brazil as a Percentage of Brazilian GDP

Year	FDI (USD Billions)	Percentage of GDP
2012	65.3	2.7*
2011	66.7	2.7
2010	48.4	2.3
2009	25.9	1.6
2008	45.1	2.8
2007	34.6	2.6
2006	18.8	1.7
2005	15.1	1.7
2004	18.1	2.7
2003	10.1	1.8

*Estimated.

Source: Central Bank of Brazil.

For more information on investing in Brazil, contact the Brazilian Trade and Investment Promotion Agency, ApexBrasil: http://www.apexbrasil.com.br.

In: Brazil: Conditions, Issues and U.S. Relations ISBN: 978-1-63321-253-4
Editor: Julia Sutton

Chapter 5

TESTIMONY OF THOMAS F. MCLARTY, CHAIRMAN, MCLARTY ASSOCIATES. HEARING ON "U.S.-BRAZIL TRADE AND INVESTMENT RELATIONSHIP: OPPORTUNITIES AND CHALLENGES"*

INTRODUCTION

Chairman Nunes, Members of the Committee – I want to thank you for hosting this hearing today on Brazil and the growing bilateral relationship.

My interest and involvement in Brazil and the Americas began a number of years before I came to Washington to serve in the Clinton administration. My older son Mark lived and worked in Brazil before attending college, and during our visits to see him, my wife and I were impressed and charmed by the country, with its natural bounty, vibrant history, rich culture, and welcoming people.

Little did I know then that I would have the opportunity to participate in forging some of our nation's key policies toward our closest neighbors, from the Mexican peso recovery package to the Caribbean Basin Initiative to Plan Colombia; or that I would have the opportunity to help shape the Summit of the Americas in 1994 in Miami – the first gathering of hemispheric leaders

* This is an edited, reformatted and augmented version of testimony presented June 12, 2013 before the House Committee on Ways and Means, Subcommittee on Trade.

since 1967; or that I would represent the United States at the signing of the Guatemala peace accords that ended a 36-year civil war.

Little did I know that I would return to the region more than 50 times as President Clinton's Special Envoy for the Americas, or that I would continue traveling Pan-American highways in the private sector through my strategic advisory firm, McLarty Associates.

So it's a pleasure and privilege to share my observations with you this morning.

A Good Moment to be Focusing on Brazil

This hearing is timely, coming on the heels of Vice President Biden's trip to Brazil just over two weeks ago, and just a few months prior to President Dilma Rousseff's State Visit in October.

As you know, this will be the first State Visit for a Brazilian President since the United States hosted President Fernando Henrique Cardoso in 1995 during my tenure in the Clinton Administration; and after 18 years, both our countries—and indeed the world—have changed.

Brazil's rise, together with that of other emerging markets such as China and India, has irreversibly shifted global dynamics.

The sharpened focus on Brazil—and, more broadly, the renewed emphasis on Latin America we are witnessing during President Obama's second term—reflects the importance of Brazil's peaceful emergence on the global stage.

Without neglecting the geopolitical hotspots critical to our national security, the United States has much to gain from new and more productive engagement with Brazil. With that in mind, I want to outline four areas of strategic cooperation with real potential for win-win outcomes—by which I mean job growth and economic prosperity for all our citizens: energy; democracy, peacekeeping and defense; China; and trade and investment.

Energy

First, energy.

The enthusiasm surrounding Brazil's discovery of enormous pre-salt oil deposits off its coast has been tempered by the acknowledgement that deep-water drilling remains a difficult and risky endeavor. The United States' significant technological and operational safety expertise could be coupled with Brazilian know-how to produce meaningful results. Chevron and Exxon Mobil participated in the 11th oil and gas bidding round conducted by the Brazilian authorities in May; but more can be done to further our technical and commercial cooperation in deep-water exploration and production.

In addition, Brazil—like the United States—is rich in shale gas reserves. Mirroring the U.S. experience, Brazil is presently struggling to enact effective regulatory regimes that balance environmental concerns with the potential of this energy resource. As Chairman Nunes is aware, a Brazilian congressional and business delegation recently visited the U.S. to learn about the U.S. experience, highlighting the potential for deeper bilateral collaboration in this area.

Lastly, and thanks in part to this Committee's leadership in lifting the ethanol tariff, our two countries can more aggressively pursue business opportunities in ethanol production, as well as jointly create development opportunities for production in third markets such as Africa or Central America and the Caribbean, where the United States and Brazil have a shared legacy and mutual desire to support human and economic development.

DEMOCRACY, PEACEKEEPING AND DEFENSE

The second area ripe for cooperation is democracy, peacekeeping and defense.

Though Brazil's cultural tendency towards non-intervention can limit the depth of our cooperation on issues such as non-proliferation, Brazil has been a steadfast peacekeeping partner in places like Haiti and the Democratic Republic of the Congo, and is seeking to increase its influence in the developing world. Brazil's Jungle Warfare Instruction Center has become an elite training center for special operations forces for African and even French and American soldiers, reflecting Brazil's desire to raise its military profile abroad.

Brazil recognizes that its newfound prominence requires a more strategic approach to defense cooperation and force modernization. To this end, in 2010, the United States and Brazil signed a Defense Cooperation Agreement to exchange defense and operational expertise. Beyond the commercial benefits, the agreement is helping Brazil enhance its military capabilities; and from the U.S. perspective, we are cementing a strategic relationship with the most culturally and politically compatible of the BRIC emerging markets—an anchor of regional stability, and a potential partner on global security issues.

While Brazil is not likely to publicly press countries over their internal political processes—as recently demonstrated by its handling of Venezuela's recent presidential election—Brazil's recognition of its role as a global leader has it focused as never before on regional stability, particularly in South America. In a shift from even a decade ago, the Brazilian government is more actively engaging in commercial diplomacy and pressing for the rule of law in countries like Ecuador and Bolivia. This trend is almost certainly correlated with the increasing presence of Brazilian multinational companies invested in the region.

CHINA

The third area for enhanced cooperation concerns China.

Both Brazil and the United States have much to gain from China's rise, as millions of new consumers enter the marketplace, offering an opportunity for companies to fill gaps that meet local needs. Brazil also serves a model for much of the developing world as it undergoes the successful integration of more than 20 million people into its middle class. My family's fourth-generation automotive enterprise has dealerships in both Brazil and China, and I can testify to the economic transformation and vast potential for business in these markets.

At the same time, both the United States and Brazil fear what China's rise might mean for domestic competitiveness. The United States has much to gain from collaborating with Brazil on approaches to China that encourage the emergence of China not only as a global giant, but also as a global stakeholder. For example, encouraging China's active participation in ensuring a more balanced and stable international monetary system.

TRADE AND INVESTMENT

The last area of mutual potential benefit that I want to highlight is trade and investment.

Since 2006, goods and services exports from the United States to Brazil have more than doubled, from $26.6 billion in 2006 to $62.7 billion in 2011.

In addition, the United States has long been one of the largest investors in Brazil.

Increasingly, however, we are seeing Brazilian firms in sectors from agriculture to steel expanding aggressively throughout the United States. USTR reports that Brazil FDI in the United States was $5 billion in 2011, up 266 percent from 2010. Portuguese is now spoken in the Great Plains, with JBS investments in Colorado, Minnesota, Nebraska and Iowa. Embraer's two plants in Jacksonville and Melbourne, Florida, will produce many of the 30 regional jets recently purchased by United Airlines, creating high-skilled jobs in those communities. Investments like these give Brazil an unprecedented stake in the U.S. economy. We should encourage the U.S. and Brazilian government to involve more closely the private sector in both countries in strategic and commercial dialogues.

The United States and Brazil also have much to gain from multilateral liberalization in agricultural trade. The WTO Doha Development Round collapsed in part because of a failure to address agricultural subsidies and domestic supports in a significant way, as well as emerging markets' reluctance to liberalize trade industrial products and services. As the United States pursues our current ambitious trade agenda in Asia and Europe, we should bear in mind that Brazil could help to bridge the longstanding North-South disputes that have stalled Doha's conclusion, even more so with a Brazilian leading the WTO. While bilateral trade and investment flows are robust, both countries are leaving money on the table by failing to deepen what could be an even more vigorous and expansive economic relationship.

CONCLUSION

Mr. Chairman, for many years and for many reasons, Brazil has been a secondary focus for U.S. foreign policy. Today, however, our neighbor's rising role, not just regionally but globally, creates an opportunity for our two nations to work together in shaping a future for the global community that reflects our democratic values and beliefs.

With the momentum created by the upcoming State Visit, and building on the spectacular tenure and professionalism of our departing U.S. Ambassador to Brazil, Tom Shannon, the moment is ripe and the stage is set for seizing that opportunity now.

High-level U.S. engagement and commitment will be essential to realize the promising opportunities I've outlined here. I am encouraged by the leadership you have shown with this hearing, and I look forward to answering any questions you may have.

Thank you.

In: Brazil: Conditions, Issues and U.S. Relations ISBN: 978-1-63321-253-4
Editor: Julia Sutton

Chapter 6

TESTIMONY OF ANDRES R. GLUSKI, CHIEF EXECUTIVE OFFICER, AES CORPORATION. HEARING ON "U.S.-BRAZIL TRADE AND INVESTMENT RELATIONSHIP: OPPORTUNITIES AND CHALLENGES"*

Chairman Nunes and distinguished Members of the Subcommittee, my name is Andrés Gluski. I am the President and Chief Executive Officer of The AES Corporation (NYSE: AES), a Fortune 200 company managing electric sector companies in many countries around the world. I am also one of the 10 U.S. members of the 2011–2013 U.S.–Brazil CEO Forum as Brazil is one of the key markets for AES. We have enjoyed a positive working relationship with the Brazilian government and we are committed to growing our business in the country. Thank you for inviting me to testify before the Subcommittee on the important topic of the trade relationship between the United States and Brazil.

AES AND ITS BRAZILIAN OPERATIONS

AES is a global power company that owns and operates a diverse and growing portfolio of electricity generation and distribution businesses. We

* This is an edited, reformatted and augmented version of testimony presented June 12, 2013 before the House Committee on Ways and Means, Subcommittee on Trade.

employ approximately 25,000 people globally, and safely provide reliable and affordable energy to customers in 25 countries. Our power plants use a broad range of technologies and fuel sources, including coal, diesel, hydropower, gas, oil, wind and biomass, and our utilities power several diverse markets, from São Paulo, Brazil to Indianapolis, Indiana. AES has a proven commitment to operational excellence in the generation and distribution of electricity to its customers. We combine our more than 30 years of experience in the field with deep local insight to provide safe and sustainable energy to improve people's lives in the markets we serve. Our success in managing a diverse fleet of energy assets across the world sustains hundreds of direct and indirect high quality finance and technical jobs at our headquarters in Arlington, Virginia.

AES has maintained an important presence in Brazil since 1997. We have invested more than $6.9 billion in the Brazilian energy sector. We hold a significant amount of our electricity generation and distribution assets in partnership with the Brazilian National Development Bank (BNDES), although AES has a controlling interest in those companies and operates them. AES Brazil is headquartered in São Paulo and currently employs more than 6,000 people. We are one of the largest electricity groups in Brazil, operating more than 3,300 MW of generation capacity and serving 7.7 million distribution customers. We control and operate two companies listed in the Sao Paulo Stock Exchange (Bovespa), Tiete and Eletropaulo, with a current combined market cap of $5 billion.

THE U.S. – BRAZIL CEO FORUM

I am honored to participate in the U.S.–Brazil CEO Forum ("the Forum"). The Forum was created in 2007 by the United States and Brazilian governments and is comprised of private and public sector representatives from both countries.

In the United States, the Forum is chaired by the U.S. Secretary of Commerce and the Deputy Assistant to the President and Deputy National Security Adviser for International Economic Affairs. In Brazil, the Forum is chaired by the President's Chief of Staff, and the Brazilian Minister of Development, Industry and Foreign Trade.

Over the past two years, the Forum's efforts have focused on improving cooperation related to issues in the areas of trade and investment, and education and innovation. We have also concentrated on the aviation, infrastructure and energy sectors.

Opportunities in the Energy Sector

At AES, we see tremendous potential for the U.S. and Brazil to cooperate in the energy sector, and we have engaged in discussions at the Forum on several key topics within the energy industry.

Development of the shale gas resource in Brazil could become a significant contributor to growth in the Brazilian economy. The Brazilian Oil Agency, ANP, originally estimated that Brazil has 32 trillion cubic feet of natural gas reserves. Those estimates have more recently been raised significantly. They now believe five basins in the country contain potential reserves of up to 500 trillion cubic feet of shale gas. This estimate is 88 percent higher than the U.S. Energy Information Administration's estimates that Brazil has 226 trillion cubic feet of gas held in shale. With either estimate, however, the potential for gas production is significant. Brazil may offer exploration blocks that contain deposits of shale gas in these five separate basins in an auction planned for December 2013.

There is significant potential for further collaboration between the U.S. and Brazil in developing these potential shale gas reserves. To foster successful collaboration and to ensure the appropriate development of these resources, attention is needed to enhance the natural gas infrastructure in Brazil, to secure enough skilled professionals to work in the industry, and to establish appropriate incentives for property owners. I'll briefly examine each of those issues.

Enhancing Natural Gas Infrastructure

In the U.S., shale gas is fundamentally changing the country's energy outlook, providing a new source of low-cost natural gas for domestic consumption and exports. The U.S.–Brazil CEO Forum believes Brazil would also benefit from growing its natural gas usage to diversify and increase the reliability of the country's energy supply while stimulating other sectors of the

Brazilian economy. Natural gas is also cheaper than other hydrocarbons and has lower CO_2 emissions.

To fully leverage its available natural gas resources, Brazil should support new investment in the development of gas transportation infrastructure. A well-organized gas transportation infrastructure will allow natural gas to be utilized widely across Brazil's vast territory.

Securing Skilled Professionals

To develop a vibrant natural gas industry, Brazil will need skilled labor to build the supporting infrastructure. In the U.S., there is uniquely skilled labor in this sector which could be leveraged to assist in efforts to further develop this industry in Brazil. If Brazil were to establish a formal Visa Waiver Program for skilled professionals, these workers could be more readily available.

For Brazil to develop its next generation of skilled labor, the nation needs policies to sponsor additional education in science, technology, engineering and math. Moreover, programs to promote internships within the private sector will also help develop the next generation of skilled labor.

The private sector can collaborate with both governments to drive education and innovation, increase job opportunities, promote economic growth and help reduce poverty.

Establishing Incentives for Property Owners

In developing natural resources, it is helpful to provide incentives to property owners for them to be able to participate in the benefits of utilizing these resources. In the United States, underlying shale gas is the property of the landowner, creating a financial incentive for private owners to allow shale gas operations and their associated disruptions to occur on their land.

In Brazil, the Federal Union generally owns the gas, not the landowner. Brazil will need to develop mechanisms to compensate and incentivize landowners to cooperate with natural resource development on their lands if the potential for the natural gas industry in Brazil is to be realized.

Sugar Based Ethanol

A closely related area where there can be significant complementarity between the U.S. and Brazil is in the area of bio-ethanol products. Brazil is the largest producer of sugar based bio-ethanol in the world, representing around 40% of its domestic fuel demand in 2012. The U.S. could benefit by loosening barriers to the import of lower cost bio-ethanol from Brazil while U.S. companies which lead in the material science discipline could benefit from favorable treatment in Brazil that would allow them access to ample supplies of economic raw materials which are not always available in North America.

Liberalizing Local Content Rules

The challenges and the opportunities that the energy sector offers to Brazil will require the cooperation of many countries to support further development. The United States is well-positioned to provide know-how in the development of oil and gas infrastructure at competitive costs, provided there is a level playing field where U.S. companies are held to the same rules applied to their Brazilian competitors.

Brazil has some of the most demanding local content laws in the world. Awarded contracts require that activities in the oil exploration phase use between 37 and 85 percent local goods and services. In the development phase, the requirement is between 55 and 80 percent.

State-owned Petrobras recently requested that regulators relax strict requirements on local content laws. Petrobras asked for these changes to be included in the next bidding rounds for new oil and gas exploration concessions in 2013. These changes will help continue development of the sector in Brazil. In addition, promoting partnerships with U.S. companies in this area, along with access to competitive Brazilian financing for U.S. investors, could significantly advance the agenda in the sector.

These local content rules are not only an issue in the energy sector, but also present challenges in other sectors as well.

INCREASING ROLE OF LOCAL CAPITAL MARKETS

The Brazilian National Development Bank (BNDES or "the Bank") plays a critical role in Brazil's current economic growth and development. The country has an agenda for the completion of significant infrastructure projects under the Growth Acceleration Program, in addition to construction of infrastructure and facilities for the 2014 FIFA World Cup and the 2016 Olympics. The Bank is the leading long-term provider of financial support for key strategic sectors in Brazil.

The Bank offers several financial support mechanisms to Brazilian companies of all sizes, as well as public administration entities in Brazil. The Bank has grown to become the largest development bank in Latin America and the second largest development bank in the world. Only the China Development Bank is larger. In 2010, the Bank had a loan portfolio three times larger than that of the World Bank and in 2012 lent more money than the World Bank and the Inter-American Development Bank combined.

The Bank supports the creation of national champions in key sectors of the Brazilian economy, such as aviation, commodities, oil and gas, poultry, meatpacking and others. This support has created Brazilian global players in different sectors of the economy that are capable of competing outside of Brazil. These companies include Petrobras, Vale, JBS and Embraer, the world's third largest aircraft manufacturer and a Brazilian member of the U.S.–Brazil CEO Forum. These companies are executing an internationalization program focused on extending their presence to become global players. They have attracted investors in local and international capital markets. Embraer's aviation business exemplifies the potential for complementarities between the two countries as Embraer's planes are manufactured in Brazil, while much of the avionics and many of the turbines are made in the United States.

Globalization and the demand for goods and services from developed markets have increased the attractiveness of local capital markets. More and more of these companies are able to raise funds in Brazil, attracting a diverse source of investors. Brazil's Securities, Commodities & Futures Exchange ranks among the world's leading exchanges by market capitalization and second in the Americas with a market capitalization for 365 companies of more than $1.22 trillion as of April 2013.

Brazilian players have been in the headlines for large transactions in many parts of the world. Recently, Jorge Paulo Lemann , a Brazilian investor with a controlling stake in Anheuser-Busch InBev, the world's largest beer company, together with his longtime partners Marcel Telles and Carlos Sicupira, made headlines, when their investment firm, 3G Capital, partnered with Warren Buffett in a $28 billion takeover of the U.S. consumer giant Heinz.

The potential is well demonstrated for the development of a deep and sophisticated capital market in Brazil. This potential must be realized if Brazil's true economic potential is to be realized.

CREATING U.S. JOB OPPORTUNITIES

The U.S. has the opportunity to create jobs both through investment in Brazil and by encouraging Brazilian investments in the U.S. We see large U.S. corporations committing to develop facilities in Brazil. Automobile manufacturers and large conglomerates such as General Electric are good examples of entities bringing competitive U.S. technology and know-how to Brazil, and at the same time increasing value for U.S. companies in their supply chains.

As an example, the GE technology center located in Rio de Janeiro develops wind turbines specifically designed for the intensity and height of Brazilian winds. This GE activity can also help bring U.S. components from other companies to Brazil as part of GE's supply chain. This approach generates jobs in the U.S., both in management of overseas assets as well as the manufacturing jobs created when U.S. components are purchased.

The U.S. and Brazil could also benefit from encouraging Brazilian investment in the U.S. infrastructure sector. Brazil has developed strong engineering and construction companies that are competing in the U.S., Latin America and Africa. The U.S. is second only to China in public ownership of its infrastructure. A widespread infrastructure privatization program promoting privatization of toll roads, highways, bridges, and ports, could represent a huge opportunity to attract Brazilian and other global investors to the U.S. infrastructure sector. Through this effort, we will be able to improve and modernize U.S. infrastructure without increasing the fiscal deficit, while also creating jobs in the construction and infrastructure sectors that could help the U.S. continue reactivating its economy. This program could benefit significantly from the work already performed by the Infrastructure committee at the U.S.–Brazil CEO Forum. The committee has already prepared documents explaining the Brazilian government's procurement policies for contracting infrastructure projects as well as detailing examples from the U.S. on a variety of public works and infrastructure contracts.

CORPORATE TAX STRUCTURE IMPROVEMENTS

Accelerating economic growth and cross-border investment between the U.S. and Brazil also requires tax certainty and tax incentives which seek to promote the domestic growth agendas of each nation. These objectives may be accomplished primarily by advancing long ongoing negotiations in support of a Bilateral Tax Treaty between the U.S. and Brazil. In the longer term, U.S. Tax Reform is needed to simplify the treatment of foreign earnings for U.S. based corporations while providing a level playing field with multi-nationals based in other jurisdictions, particularly in Europe and Asia.

Building on the success of the recently approved U.S./Brazil Tax Information Exchange Agreement, we support the re-initiation of negotiations on the terms of a Bilateral Tax Treaty to reduce or eliminate double taxation and provide economic incentives to stimulate cross border investment and job creation opportunities. Such incentives, including reduced rates of withholding tax on interest, dividends, royalties, and payments for technical services would be mutually beneficial to both U.S. and Brazilian investors and would improve overall investment efficiency between the two nations.

We also support comprehensive tax reform in the U.S. that seeks to simplify and modernize the corporate tax system by introducing a competitive territorial tax system that eliminates the current disadvantage U.S. companies face relative to their foreign competitors. In an era of extraordinary capital mobility, tax reform provides an opportunity to make U.S. multi-nationals more competitive on a global scale and the U.S. a more attractive investment locale. These changes would spur job creation and domestic economic growth by encouraging U.S. companies to repatriate cash to the United States.

Investment firms such as AES require certainty over the U.S. taxation of foreign earnings which are actively managed. A leader in this field, AES has successfully tapped into local capital markets for more than a decade to raise equity in support of its business growth objectives through its controlled foreign corporations and seeks certainty that income derived from these actively managed equity market investments will continue to benefit from U.S. tax deferral, consistent with the U.S. tax treatment of investments structured through private party ventures. To state it simply, with growing local capital markets, it does not make economic sense to discriminate in any way from a tax perspective between those companies using publicly listed controlled foreign corporations to raise capital abroad versus private partnerships or private joint ventures. The former help better integrate U.S. companies into the national fabric of the countries where they operate while providing greater transparency and governance.

TRADE AGREEMENTS

In addition to the specific policy issues already identified, both governments should be encouraged to reach a long-term trade and investment liberalization framework. Brazil and the U.S. both supported the Doha negotiations; however, a positive outcome currently seems distant. Due to the fact that a multilateral agreement seems unlikely, several bilateral agreements have been implemented among many of our major trading partners. Both nations should take note of increasing shifts in trade and investment flows from the Atlantic to the Pacific. In response, the United States and Brazil should seek a fully integrated economic area within this hemisphere. Realizing this opportunity will create an environment for job and wealth creation, a priority our countries share. As President Obama said during his presidential visit to Rio in March 2011, "together we can advance our common prosperity." Let's continue on this path of mutual collaboration in a bilateral trade and investment relationship.

CONCLUSION

I appreciate the opportunity to present this testimony to the committee. Thank you for your time and consideration.

In: Brazil: Conditions, Issues and U.S. Relations ISBN: 978-1-63321-253-4
Editor: Julia Sutton

Chapter 7

STATEMENT OF ROBERTO MARQUES, COMPANY GROUP CHAIRMAN, JOHNSON & JOHNSON CONSUMER COMPANIES OF NORTH AMERICA. HEARING ON "U.S.-BRAZIL TRADE AND INVESTMENT RELATIONSHIP: OPPORTUNITIES AND CHALLENGES"*

Thank you, Chairman Nunes, Ranking Member Rangel, and distinguished members of the House Ways and Means Subcommittee on Trade for allowing me the opportunity to testify today. My name is Roberto Marques, and I am the Company Group Chairman for the Johnson & Johnson Consumer Companies of North America.

ABOUT THE COUNCIL AND THE CHAMBER

I am honored to testify today on behalf of the U.S. Section of the Brazil-U.S. Business Council (BUSBC). BUSBC is the premier business advocacy organization dedicated to strengthening the economic and commercial relationship between the United States and Brazil. BUSBC was established in

* This is an edited, reformatted and augmented version of a statement presented June 12, 2013 before the House Committee on Ways and Means, Subcommittee on Trade.

1976. It is the oldest and largest bilateral private sector group focusing on the U.S.-Brazil commercial relationship. I am especially honored because I am from Brazil, and it is my passion to do my part in building cooperation between two great countries.

BUSBC is comprised of two sections. The U.S. Section represents more than 100 major U.S. companies with investments and businesses in Brazil. Johnson & Johnson is proud to serve on the board of directors of the U.S. Section of BUSBC. The Brazil Section represents Brazilian companies and trade associations with investments and businesses in the United States. It is housed in the Brazilian National Confederation of Industry (CNI) and is chaired by Embraer.

BUSBC also works in conjunction with the American Chamber of Commerce for Brazil (in São Paulo), the American Chamber of Commerce in Rio de Janeiro, the U.S.-Brazil CEO Forum, and sectoral associations in both countries. This structure enables BUSBC to forge consensus between the two private sectors and communicate to both governments with a unique bilateral voice.

The U.S. Section of the BUSBC is an affiliate of the U.S. Chamber of Commerce. The Chamber is the world's largest business federation, representing the interests of more than three million businesses of all sizes, sectors, and regions, as well as state and local chambers and industry associations, and dedicated to promoting, protecting and defending America's free enterprise system. Its International Affairs division includes more than 50 regional and policy experts and 25 country- and region-specific business councils and initiatives.

About Johnson & Johnson

Johnson & Johnson has approximately 127,600 employees worldwide engaged in the research and development, manufacture and sale of a broad range of products in the health care field. The Company conducts business in virtually all countries of the world with the primary focus on products related to human health and well-being. Research and development activities represent a significant part of our business, and last year we spent over $7.5 billion worldwide, $4.0 billion of that amount in the U.S. Those research dollars help support, among other things, 3,763 clinical trials on new and life-improving pharmaceuticals and are being conducted with the enrollment of 183,200 patients at 8,465 trial sites.

The Company is organized into three business segments: Consumer, Pharmaceutical and Medical Devices and Diagnostics. The Consumer segment, which I lead in North America, includes a broad range of products used in the baby care, skin care, oral care, wound care and women's health fields, as well as nutritional and over-the-counter pharmaceutical products and wellness and prevention platforms. The Pharmaceutical segment includes products in the following areas: anti-infective, antipsychotic, contraceptive, gastrointestinal, hematology, immunology, infectious diseases, neurology, oncology, pain management, thrombosis and vaccines. The Medical Device and Diagnostics segment includes a broad range of products to treat cardiovascular disease; orthopedic and neurological products; blood glucose monitoring and insulin delivery products; general surgery, biosurgical and energy products; professional diagnostic products; infection prevention products; and disposable contact lenses.

Johnson & Johnson makes an important contribution to the U.S. economy. We have 48,000 direct jobs in the U.S. which in turn help support 254,700 indirect jobs, which means for every one direct job in the U.S., we support 5.3 additional jobs in the U.S. economy. Similarly, for every dollar of Johnson & Johnson output, we add 1.4 dollars in additional indirect output in the U.S. economy.

We are also very proud of our company's presence in Brazil where we have operated for 80 years. Johnson & Johnson's sales in Brazil are almost $2 billion per year with an estimated 20% operational growth. We are committed to Brazil and have made substantial investments there that support 6,000 direct and 25,600 indirect jobs.

Our major facilities are at the São José dos Campos Industrial Park which makes a variety of products including toiletries, dental hygiene products, needles, sutures, and over-the-counter drugs. The Johnson & Johnson Consumer R&D Center in Brazil employs 180 scientists. We have research and development activities in Brazil including 35 clinical trials, enrolling 5,135 patients and 1,556 health professional at 152 sites. We very much view our relationship with Brazil as one that benefits both the U.S. and Brazilian economies as well as consumers, patients, and ultimately our company.

Progress and Prospects for Bilateral Commerce

As the world's seventh largest economy, Brazil has become a vital market for U.S. companies. Growing trade, significant oil discoveries, financial stability, low inflation, rising investment, a booming middle class, and political stability are some of the factors that have contributed to Brazil's rise as a prosperous and influential country on the world stage.

U.S.-Brazil trade has seen significant progress in recent years. U.S. merchandise exports to Brazil reached $43.7 billion last year, representing an increase of more than 250 percent over the past decade. Brazil's growing middle class has made it an attractive market for U.S. exporters and for U.S. investors, many of which are in sectors (such as services) that can only access the local market by means of a local presence.

However, it is clear that U.S. and Brazilian firms have barely tapped the possibilities of this relationship. Brazil's market is far more open to imports than it was 15 years ago, but its tariffs and other barriers are on average significantly higher than those of most other middle income economies. Reflecting this reality, most foreign investment in Brazil is focused on reaching its large domestic market and is not intended to leverage Brazil's potential as an export platform.

This situation is not changing as global trade talks advance. Today, the United States is undertaking ambitious negotiations with major markets in the Trans-Pacific Partnership (TPP) and Trans-Atlantic Trade and Investment Partnership (TTIP). These "mega-regional" trade negotiations will encompass a majority of the world's purchasing power, magnifying their potential commercial value. In Geneva, negotiations are now underway for a Trade in Services Agreement (TISA) that aims to establish a high-standard free-trade agreement among nearly 50 countries, and hopes are high that negotiators will conclude talks to expand the product coverage of the highly successful Information Technology Agreement (ITA) within months.

Unfortunately, Brazil is not yet participating in these negotiations. The Council considers this a lost opportunity because Brazil is home to dynamic, innovative companies with tremendous competitive advantages based on its human capital and natural resources, as well as its strong democracy.

Changing Views in Brazil

There are signs this may be changing. Brazil's agricultural sector, which is among the world's most competitive, long ago adopted an outward-looking orientation and has focused on the country's vast possibilities as an exporter. Brazilian agribusiness leaders argue forcefully that the country will benefit greatly if it can win improved access to foreign markets. In addition, Brazil's services market is relatively open and competitive.

The manufacturing sector's views may be changing as well. Brazil's National Confederation of Industry (CNI) has suggested it is dissatisfied with the way Mercosul has held Brazil back from undertaking external trade negotiations. Brazil's Federation of Industries of the State of São Paulo (FIESP), has echoed this dissatisfaction with Mercosul, suggested that Brazil's internal market may be insufficient to guarantee its future, and has indicated that Brazil should explore the possibility of negotiating market-opening trade agreements bilaterally.

In this sense, the United States is an obvious partner. While China has overtaken the United States as an export market for Brazil, Chinese imports from Brazil are dominated by raw materials such as iron ore and soybeans. In contrast, the United States is a key market for the export of Brazil's value-added products, making the United States an important partner in efforts by Brazilian firms to climb the value chain. Towards that end, BUSBC sees as important Congressional action for the renewal of the U.S. Generalized System of Preferences, a key program for Brazilian exports to the United States. Global value chains do not connect the United States and Brazil as tightly as the United States and Mexico or China and Japan, for instance, but they are significant in some sectors, such as aerospace, and offer a platform for further growth.

Brazil's vigorous and successful campaign in favor of the selection of its native son Roberto Azevêdo as the next Director-General of the World Trade Organization (WTO) is a sign that Brazil aspires to be a leader in international trade issues (while acknowledging that the highly regarded Azevêdo will represent the interests of all 159 WTO Members once he assumes his new role on September 1). This was also underscored by a Brazilian agriculture proposal at the WTO last fall (relating to the administration of tariff-rate quotas) that the United States praised as helpful in building support for a package of tangible deliverables at the WTO's 9th Ministerial Conference scheduled to be held in Bali, Indonesia, in December.

In sum, Brazil's private sector is emerging as a voice in favor of closer trade ties — and new trade agreements — with other nations, including the United States. The Brazilian government's efforts to push forward negotiations at the WTO are positive as well. Perhaps the ground has been prepared for Brazil to assume new ambitions in its international trade and investment policies befitting its emergence on the world stage.

THE COUNCIL'S POLICY PRIORITIES

BUSBC has labored for years to facilitate U.S. companies' access to the Brazilian market via strategic policy deliverables. Of the many issues that BUSBC works on, I am here today to speak on three of our top priorities regarding the bilateral relationship. They are the launching of talks on a *Bilateral Economic Partnership Agreement*, the starting of negotiations on a *Bilateral Tax Treaty*, and *visa-free, entry-facilitated travel.*

a) Bilateral Economic Partnership Agreement

Since the visit of Brazilian President Dilma Rousseff to the United States in April 2012, BUSBC has been actively promoting an all-encompassing bilateral trade agreement known informally as a Bilateral Economic Partnership Agreement. Today there is consensus between the U.S. Section and the Brazil Section of BUSBC on the need to explore such a partnership. This consensus opens the door for a more structured discussion with the Brazilian private sector and the U.S. and Brazilian governments.

Why pursue such an agreement? First and foremost, U.S.-Brazil trade in goods and services of $100 billion annually is still far from its potential. As Vice President Joseph Biden said in his recent trip to Brazil, "There's no reason why that cannot be $400 billion to $500 billion a year." Second, such an agreement could also boost two-way foreign direct investment flow to a more significant level. The stock of U.S. foreign direct investment in Brazil was $71.1 billion in 2011, up 10.8% from 2010. Brazilian foreign direct investment in the United States was $5.0 billion in 2011, up 266% from 2010. A Bilateral Economic Partnership Agreement would provide greater predictability and confidence to investors in both countries. With so much to gain on both sides, we hope Congress will support further exploration of this proposal.

b) A Bilateral Tax Treaty

BUSBC's second priority is the launching of negotiations for a Bilateral Tax Treaty. This would provide for the elimination of double taxation, the reduction and/or elimination of taxes on royalties, interests, and dividends, and the establishment of a dispute settlement mechanism. Brazil is the largest market in the world with which the United States has not negotiated such an agreement, and doing so would spur growth and job creation in both countries.

On that front, we applaud the Brazilian Senate's approval earlier this year of the 2007 U.S-Brazil Tax Information Exchange Agreement (TIEA). This agreement will greatly facilitate cooperation between the Brazilian Federal Revenue Service and the Internal Revenue Service, and by some measures makes the negotiation of a Bilateral Tax Treaty much easier. With the TIEA approved, there is an opportunity for the U.S. and Brazilian private sectors to advocate for the launching of formal Bilateral Tax Treaty negotiations. The upcoming State Visit of President Rousseff to Washington in October should create additional momentum in securing this goal, and we urge Congress to lend its support as well.

c) Visa-Free and Entry-Facilitated Travel

BUSBC advocates for entry-facilitated and ultimately visa-free travel between the United States and Brazil. To that end, BUSBC efforts focus on two complementary goals: the inclusion of Brazil in the U.S. Visa Waiver Program and in the U.S. Global Entry program. In both cases, we strongly support reciprocal actions by Brazil. One example of progress in this area is Brazil's newly created expedited process for issuance of visas to temporary workers. This action will facilitate the entry of U.S. high-skilled workers on assignment in Brazil.

Visa-free travel is a win-win for both countries. Brazilians are among the highest-spending visitors to the United States in terms of outlays per traveler. The number of Brazilians visiting the United States has quadrupled since 2004, reaching 1.5 million in 2011, according to the U.S. Department of Commerce. Their total expenditures that year reached $8.5 billion, or more than $5,600 per visitor. Visa-free travel would multiply these visitors and the growth-driving, job-creating benefits it provides for the U.S. hospitality industry.

From the perspective of U.S. business and leisure travelers, the upcoming soccer World Cup and Olympic Games to be held in Brazil are likely to attract millions of U.S. tourists who would benefit from visa-free entry into Brazil. Visa-free travel would also be valuable for the many business people and temporary workers who travel frequently between the U.S. and Brazil. I must add that reflecting our deep involvement in Brazilian society, Johnson & Johnson is also proud to be the exclusive and official healthcare sponsor of the 2014 FIFA World Cup BrazilTM, the first health care company to be so honored in the history of the competition.

Deepening the Partnership through Dialogue

Brazil and the United States have a long history of positive relations. This relationship has strengthened in recent years, as demonstrated by high-level policy mechanisms between the two countries and the frequency of presidential meetings. There are approximately 30 dialogues between the two countries that involve key government agencies and both countries. Of all the dialogues in place, four of them are Presidential-level dialogues: the Global Partnership Dialogue (2010), the Strategic Energy Dialogue (2011), the Economic and Financial Dialogue (2011), and the more recent Defense Cooperation Dialogue (2012).

BUSBC stresses the importance of private sector participation in these dialogues. Such participation exists in the Strategic Energy Dialogue, the Commercial Dialogue, and the ICT and Internet Policy Dialogue. BUSBC has consistently seen positive results from such interaction. Ideally, we would like to duplicate the channels of communication created by the various government-to-government dialogues in the private sector. For that to happen, BUSBC advocates for formal participation of the private sector in all the dialogues and working groups already created by both governments.

While there is a great deal of potential in Brazil, speaking as a representative of one of the world's largest health care companies, I must also note the importance of strengthened intellectual property rights protection, internationally consistent procedures for patent review, and an open and transparent regulatory process. We must be able to discuss our differences as well as our commonalities if we wish to have a truly productive bilateral relationship. If Brazil hopes to become a leader in innovation, it must be certain that is adequately protecting innovators.

One Roadblock: The Cotton Dispute

I would like to highlight one important issue vis-à-vis bettering the Brazil-U.S. trade relationship: the U.S.-Brazil cotton dispute. BUSBC, through its leadership role in the Brazil Trade Action Coalition, known as BRAZTAC, has worked with both governments and the U.S. Congress to deter WTO-sanctioned retaliation by Brazil relating to the cotton dispute — which could impact U.S. goods, services, and intellectual property valued as high as $1 billion by some estimates — and to encourage a definitive resolution to the dispute since 2010. BRAZTAC is comprised of a broad range of U.S. agricultural, manufacturing, services, and technology businesses and trade associations that support a solution to prevent Brazilian trade retaliation against U.S. goods and intellectual property rights.

Such a definitive resolution of the dispute is within reach. We trust that the U.S. Congress will pass a 2013 Farm Bill that brings the United States into compliance with its WTO obligations relating to this dispute, thus removing the risk of WTO-sanctioned trade retaliation against U.S. exports and intellectual property. It is important that the United States lead by example, and only by meeting our own trade obligations can we effectively urge all other countries to similarly meet their trade obligations. In the meantime, we appeal to Congress to maintain the temporary framework agreement that has deferred retaliation until the Farm Bill is passed.

CONCLUSION

We have achieved significant progress in the bilateral relationship between United States and Brazil. This progress has been gradual and steady, from the recent approval of the Tax Information Exchange Agreement by Brazil to the elimination of the ethanol tariff by the United States and many other accomplishments. In the near term, President Rousseff's State Visit should provide an opportunity to advance talks on a Bilateral Tax Treaty, Brazil's inclusion in the Global Entry Program, and the approval of various bilateral agreements that have yet to be ratified by the Brazilian Congress.

Other areas where the BUSBC is pressing for improvements in Brazil's business climate include harmonization and transparency in the rule-making process, protection of intellectual property, and the minimization of local content regulations in various sectors within Brazil. In the long run, we see great potential in partnerships between the two countries in the areas of energy, defense and security, and ICT and Internet policy.

We greatly appreciate the efforts of this Subcommittee in organizing this hearing and honing congressional leadership on U.S.-Brazil trade issues. BUSBC is at the disposal of the Subcommittee to work on issues relating to trade and investment between the United States and Brazil. Likewise, we reiterate our desire to continue to work closely with the Brazil Caucus in its mission to foster understanding and enhance the U.S. relationship with Brazil.

Thank you for this opportunity. I look forward to your questions.

INDEX

C

D

E

F

G

H

I

P

T

U

V

W

X

Y